THE
AMERICAN
REVOLUTION

By
Don De Angelo

Preface
(If I Were the King of the Forrest)

It's the title of my favorite song from the "Wizard of Oz." Ever since childhood I have identified with the cowardly lion. He's strong enough and powerful enough but so much self-doubt has entered his life that the only safe reaction to trouble is to flee.

So much in our lives today seems so large and daunting that we become paralyzed by doubt and fear. I have been a student of politics and international relations since 1984 when I studied for my BA at the University of Delaware. I had always been conscious of what was going on in the world, but Delaware was the first place where my ideas were challenged. I was forced to argue about my positions and opinions. The debates stirred my interest and when I finally got my chance to pursue graduate work in 1993, I entered the University of San Diego for a MA in International Relations. Then I returned to teacher. In my efforts to become as much of an expert on American history and government as possible, I ventured into the depth of literature that defines the curriculum. Finally, I was named a Fellow of the James Madison Memorial Fellowship Foundation in 2007 and given a grant to complete a MA in history.

The American Revolution

Over these years of work and study, many people have come to me and asked why I don't pursue a career in politics. Even those who might not agree with my perspectives have voiced their support. And this is when that song comes to my head. The lion sings this song because he has wonderful ideas, a sensitive nature, and a kind heart – but, he hasn't the courage to do what he feels would be necessary to get the job done. That's me all over. A king gets to say what he wants and by sheer force of will, he can get it. An American politician, for good reason, seldom has such a luxury. I have never been sure I have the patience for that reality. I certainly don't know if average Americans can handle what is in my closet, which is enough to keep me out of the spotlight.

And so, I teach. In my fear of being exposed and scrutinized in ways yet unknown, I choose to instruct the future leaders. This book is a substitute for my candidacy. I write it with the hope that it will inspire someone to try these ideas out. It is my only course of action. I have my carpet-cape and planter-pot crown on and ready to go!

Update: Preface from Olean, NY 2023

A great deal has happened since the first publication of *The American REvolution* in 2020. While the focus tends to be on the COVID-19 pandemic, it seems now that this was a mere distraction from the not-so-veiled takeover of most our personal lives by the federal government and the "deep state" more specifically.

As of May 2023, various media sources and confessions by inside whistleblowers has confirmed what many of us

Don De Angelo

liberty-minded people had suspected – and were accused of being conspiracy theorists for espousing – which was the outright fabrication of most if not all the fears sold to the world.

A pandemic created by taxpayer money without their consent was leaked to the world by a known global dictatorship (by ineptitude or malice), and the Western democracies told multiple lies to hide the truth of their complicity. Virtually the entire world put into lockdown and forced to take a vaccine that was secretly known to not be as effective as promised with now confirmed side effects which include premature death. When government becomes this bad and so incompetent, there needs to be a reckoning.

A climate crisis that is nothing of the sort is being sold to people as an "existential threat" to mankind, while real science confirms the opposite. We are being forced off meat, fossil fuels, and even our own jobs to save us from a phantom enemy that is now being exposed as a coordinated hoax. But no one is named as criminally culpable. No one is on the chopping block for prosecution or even being fired from their job. Dr. Anthony Fauci is being permitted to keep his millions of dollars earned from royalties that Americans were not told existed. It is the stuff that confirms conspiracies and empowers anarchists.

So, the cowardly lion is pushed into action. Just as in the movie, my life has been turned upside down and reinforced by my Christian and libertarian principles. When Dorothy's life was in jeopardy, the lion roared for real; and that was when he realized that he had "unrecognized" courage. The moral of Baum's original book was to remind people that injustices occur and there is more courage inside of us that we never realized.

The American Revolution

Are we all one of the characters of Oz? When do we wake up and see what we should have known all along? If there is no wizard to grant us our wishes, is the message that we will have to make things happen on our own? And is there "no place like home?"

Table of Content

Preface   3

Introduction   8

Part 1: Theo-Libertarian Citizenship   21

Part 2: The Bear-Flag Republic   57

Part 3: The National Revival   106

Part 4: Options and Choices   218

Epilogue   234

A Short Reading List   236

About the Author   238

Introduction

It was early in 2023, just after I adopted my dog Brida (Bree-Dah) but before getting my second dog, Heike (Hi-Kah). I woke up from a dead sleep screaming. Not sure about what exactly was happening, I looked over to see Brida staring at me with a "what did you just say?" look in her eyes. There wasn't a dream that I remember reacting to or a specific horror that made me scream.

I sat there for a few minutes and thought, "why would I be terrified by something I can't even remember?" But I suddenly thought about what had been on my mind for a very long time, how the whole world seemed determined to implode. With that I tried to go back to sleep but all the issues about current affairs rattled through my brain and I contented myself with lying awake for the rest of the night (Brida slept just fine if you were concerned).

While I have always been into current affairs, history, and politics, the recent three years has seen my focus become narrower and more analytical. Can anyone really explain what in the name of Samuel Clemens has happened these past three years (2020-2023)? I know I am not the only one who feels like the entire world has lost its mind. The number of rabbit holes I have traveled investigating and researching the issues confronting the

Don De Angelo

United States and the Western world in general cannot be measured in hours, but by days.

The first edition of *The American REvolution* was self-published in January of 2019, a year before the COVID 19 pandemic. Much of what I wrote then, which is not a long time in human affairs, seems naïve and perhaps irrelevant now. The immediate impact of the pandemic on me was that most people were more concerned with their impending death rather than a discussion on how to improve American politics and public affairs.

Observations of what happened during the period has led me to want a redo. While I was living in San Diego for most of the events, my personal journey one of isolation, professional and personal frustration, and intense grief. If someone were to say to me five years ago that I would endure such an odyssey, I would have given them the death stare. Looking back there were many lessons learned but also many questions unanswered.

In the winter of 2020, I was in the 24th year of teaching at a very popular Catholic high school in San Diego, California. I was renting a small cottage in La Mesa and relatively content as a single, middle-aged male. Nothing was going that great, but nothing was awful. I was floating along, planning for a typical retirement outside of California because it was clearly becoming too expensive to live in America's Finest City.

I was also the Vice-Chair of the San Diego County Libertarian Party. It sounds very important until you learn that I got the position because the previous officer simply stopped showing up and I was willing to do the work (for free). Re-election was essentially assured for the same reason. It was in this role that I wrote the first edition of *The American REvolution*. After 23 years

The American Revolution

of teaching, I had been granted a partial sabbatical, begin in the fall of 2020, to write a follow-up book, *The Bear Flag Republic*, addressing similar ideas of reform for California. Part-time work allowed me to finish the second book in just five months as opposed to the first, which took five years.

In January of 2021, my father suddenly died from COVID. I say "suddenly" because I spoke with him in the morning, and he told me that he was feeling great and that his doctor was going to release him from the hospital later that day. I left my house to run some errands and go to the gym. As I was driving home, I got an email from my stepmother saying that my dad was in ICU and that he was not going to make it. Much of that day is now a blur but I still remember feeling like the whole world fell away and I was suddenly lost. I was one of "those people" who lost someone to the pandemic. Piecing together elements of his treatment, it is evident that a multiple of known errors were made.

The first unexplainable mistake was that Pennsylvania made senior citizens wait for a vaccine while allowing some public employees, regardless of risks, cut the line. Secondly, it encouraged people to stay indoors, which depleted sunlight and the ability of one's own body to build up immunity.[1] The next inexplicable error was the denial that there were legitimate therapies to ameliorate the suffering of patients once they were infected. It is now understood that peer-reviewed studies were available lauding the use of ivermectin and monoclonal treatments to keep patients

---

1 I was chastised by a friend for not having "sources" for my *conspiracy theories* so let's start with lockdown laws. https://fortune.com/2023/06/06/ste ve-hanke-money-doctor-covid-lockdowns-policy-mistake/.

Don De Angelo

out of the hospital.[2] As alternative media digs into the data and communications, it becomes clear that established powers wanted to control both the process of dealing with the pandemic and the official narrative under which we all lived. It was more important to secure the profits of big pharma and those in the healthcare bureaucracy than to end the suffering and death of millions of people. The final insult to our collective notion of humanity, my father was given remdesivir and intubated, which essential ensured that he would die. While it should go without saying; we should recall that many Germans were executed after World War II for experimenting with non-consenting human beings.[3] No more need be added.

Because he had been denied unction of the sick or "last rites" I wanted him to have a funeral. My stepmother did not want to have one because of the restrictions due to the pandemic and concerns for logistics and safety. Pennsylvania was where everything needed to happen, so I had to plan his funeral via email and then deal with the travel and work rules of California. To accommodate all the rules and concerns, I flew to Pittsburgh on Friday night, met my niece and drove to Greensburg for over 30 minutes, got up Saturday for his viewing, funeral, and burial; and then drove to the airport to fly home, so I could be back to test on Sunday and be back a work on Monday.

---

2   Another example of the unscientific science: The BBC was THE supposed authority on treatments issued this report -- https://www.youtube.com/watch?v=H66tBH2oku4. BUT a trained medical professor proved it completely nonsensical. https://www.youtube.com/watch?v=zy7c_FHiEac

3   Here is an excellent *Reason* interview that demonstrates all the unscientific science of COVID policy. Some will criticize citing of an entire interview, but I want to be sure that I am not quoting out of context.

The American Revolution

A week after getting back, I was working at home when a friend called from the school. "Are you coming to school today?" Not knowing anything I said, "no, it's my day off." As my friend began to get choked up, she told me that one of my department colleagues, and a former student of mine, had been killed (executed really) by his fiancé's ex-boyfriend. I collapsed. I was completely unable to comprehend why this would happen. The school was in lockdown and the students, faculty, and staff were in collective shock.

This was to be a year of funerals — some 20 in all over a six-month period. It felt as though every time I read the paper or got a call from a long distant friend or relative, it was bad news. It wasn't much different from most people, but the isolation caused by the COVID lockdowns made everything worse. As a single man, I was spending nearly 90 percent of my life alone. Teaching with a mask on with half of your students present and the other half online is not the same. There is a reason why we collectively celebrate and mourn and try to learn lessons. The support felt in such events and moments reinforces a sense of connectedness and solidarity. To deny people such human warmth was severe. To do so when it was not necessary was cruel and criminal.

The inhumanity and insanity of the rules and regulations. The authoritarian methodology. It was living in an Orwell book. I became angry at the realization that power was being used in such a totalitarian way and no one seemed angry let alone concerned that our freedoms might never be restored. My good buddy, Joseph DePaul and I had been doing a podcast every week for the local Libertarian party, and we were following the statistics of the pandemic. None of the stats seem to support the draconian policies.

Don De Angelo

When does a society need to "obey" the state, and when should that same collective demand obedience from the state? A Libertarian would always say that it is always the latter. Obedience to the state is always a recipe for oppression and abuse of power. The US Constitution is premised on the notion that "we the people" determine the parameters of government power. There was never a vote. We were never asked if our lives should be upended and destroyed. The most revealing thing for me was the actual manipulation of information and curtailing of free speech. We were put through hell on purpose as an experiment in population control. The facts were kept from us, and we were not allowed to even know about contrary evidence.

But the truth got out anyway. Thank the Lord for the internet and alternative media. Millions of people around the world were able to dive into rabbit holes of data and analysis that demonstrated just how awful governments behaved and how many lives were ended, including my father's.[4]

As of the writing of this book, these are the facts so far as can be understood. The United States government, in collaboration with other developed nations and international bodies such as the World Health Organization (WHO) and the World Economic Forum (WEF) decided to study how viruses become more dangerous to humans. The gain of function research proved dangerous, and a lab accident in North Carolina prompted the Director of National Intelligence (DNI) to warn the Obama administration that any such research should be halted.

---

4   John Campbell is a British medical professor (nursing) who has done the best work on COVID statistics. If you desire to know the real science, visit his YouTube page: https://www.youtube.com/@Campbellteaching.

The American Revolution

Dr. Anthony Fauci seems to have decided this was not the correct policy decision and funneled money for the research to continue through Eco Health Alliance, which was working with a lab in Wuhan China. When the Trump administration was setting up shop in 2017, Dr. Fauci eerily announced that there would be a major pandemic during the new administration. Two years later, whether by accident or intention, a corona virus was leaked into the population. The facts as known should outrage the entire world and yet somehow the only discussion in mainstream media is that we should prepare for the next pandemic by trusting these same institutions. Others are out there insisting that we should offer forgiveness without even expressing an apology, let alone accept culpability.[5]

What transpired next can only be described as a tragedy of errors and abuses. We were told in December of 2020 that there was something happening in China but was of no concern to anyone else. Then in January 2021, it was something bad but under control and don't bother wearing a mask because it won't do any good. A month later and it was something bad and for God's sake, WEAR A MASK! Another month later and the entire world (except Sweden apparently) was in lockdown. Never mind that all the international data was indicating that it was a deadly illness for those over 65 with comorbidity issues; but not a threat to virtually anyone else. This information was ignored and denied true by the very scientists we were told to heed.

---

5 Many people refuse to accept anything from RFK, Jr. Brett Weinstein is an evolutionary biologist who did graduate work on bat viruses. This interview matters: https://www.youtube.com/watch?v=A2TPBjS5EF8. An amazing interview of Brett on UnHerd: https://www.youtube.com/watch?v=dLp9YMM7CI4.

Don De Angelo

The CDC, FDA, NIH and WHO all colluded with mainstream and social media to hide data from the public and multitudes of professional doctors and scientists were silenced, canceled, and "de-platformed." Thousands of young people were denied a proper education, some of whom will be permanently set back on their intellectual and social development. As many people were damaged by the remedy as they were by the disease.

The level of incompetence and diabolical abuse of power has been unprecedented, and no one has been held responsible. Dr. Fauci has been allowed to retire without consequence and we are now permitted to know, only because of FOIA requests by alternative media, that he had financially benefitted from the vaccines he oversaw approving and regulating throughout decades of "public service." The average American is left to wonder, "Could I get away with such behavior?"[6]

The rising popular anger about these truths is evidence that the global elite have miscalculated in their assumption that us average slobs are incapable of understanding the complexity of their *Great Reset*, let alone make a firm opinion as to the immoral reality of such activity. It appears that we common folk can sit through hours of debate and data analysis without losing our concentration if perhaps not our tempers.

If this were not bad enough. We now have whistleblowers and documented evidence that President Biden and his son Hunter may have received $10 million in bribes while Joe was Vice-President. Where was such bribery happening? Ukraine. Yes,

---

6   Great interview of Senator Dr. Rand Paul that lays out the government's deceit over COVID: https://www.youtube.com/watch?v=3I7HFriEVxQ.

The American Revolution

that country where we are now spending billions of dollars, we do not have to fight a proxy war with Russia so that our military industrial complex can continue to make billions. And yet, the global mainstream media seem completely uninterested.

I won't even get started on election fraud and all the nonsense there, except to say that there has never been an actual review of the 2020 election processes. As a person who voted for neither party, the frustrations never end for the simple fact that, if election irregularity can be so easily brushed aside, what hope does a third-party candidate have of giving agency to alternative voices. Add the awareness that while Jeffrey Epstein was arrested and JP Morgan Chase has agreed to pay money for having abetted the trafficking in minors for prostitution, not one single "client" has been named even though a "list" is in the possession of the FBI. After all the obfuscations of facts in other scandals of government malfeasance one can only assume there is some truth to those allegations.

Living in California did not make things any easier. The People's Republic of California is a case study in the perils of socialism and the evils of one-party rule. When I first moved there in 1992, it was paradise. It had problems for sure but there was a competitive political arena and a healthy economic engine. When things started to go South, around the Grey Davis governorship, I was convinced that the ship would correct itself.

Then there was the "bullet train."

Environmentalists convinced Californians that we could solve the global warming terror that was leading to our state's droughts by taking millions of cars off our freeways. Build a train from Los Angeles to San Francisco that will make the trip in just two hours, and the people will flee their cars in droves.

Don De Angelo

While this may seem a trivial issue, it underscores all that is wrong, if not sinister, that is centralized government without limitations. Once the decision was made to begin the project no amount of evidence of failure could detract from the stated goal. When the same environmentalists objected to the quickest route for the bullet train because it would violate precious wetlands and breeding grounds. The reality a two-hour trip was now to be over four did not deter the endeavor. When the promised private investments did not materialize, the only acceptable response was to beg the federal government for the money. Never mind that this was still public money and violating the original statute – this was not to be discussed.[7]

When the Obama administration agreed to send a mere fraction of the needed funds under the commitment to begin construction, the wisdom of government planning led to rails to begin in the least populated part of the new route – Bakersfield to Merced. Decades later, and billions wasted, and the lauded symbol of government largess is yet to materialize.

The conclusion made is that my first two books were not adequate to the new revelations. The need for reforming the government is now no longer needed – it is of critical importance. Failure to enact major changes risk losing the entire American enterprise. We are no longer at the luxury of choosing what to fix and what to leave alone. We have struck the iceberg and it is all hands-on deck!

The meat of this book's analysis is derived from the earlier work because it still holds true to the initial thesis, which is that

---

7   Here I am going to use a rather benign criticism: https://www.youtube.com/watch?v=S0dSm_ClcSw.

The American Revolution

the system proscribed by the US Constitution is still valid and has simply been ignored. Reenlist these concepts and use them as the template of reform and all will be well. The changes made are due to the litany of SNAFUs experienced from 2020-2023.

The book is divided into parts meant to establish the proper mentality and structure for saving the Union. **Part I** is devoted to the fundamental change that needs to take place for the United States to restore the *City on a Hill* invoked by Jonathan Winthrop and revived by Ronald Reagan. Without the inner revival of the individual and the self-reliance that builds strong people incapable of surrendering personal liberties, no other reforms of government are possible. Whether we want to accept this or not, we have become a people comfortable with taking government hand-outs. It could be a tax break or a subsidy, or the mentality that if a local project gets federal funding, we have somehow scored an advantage; that makes all of us OK with government largess.

Part II is looking at government at the state and local level. If one follows the intent of the constitution, the state was meant to be the main source of daily government presence. Most of the states in 1787 feared the idea of surrendering all their power to a distant, central government. Therefore, the framework of American government was decentralized except in matters deemed purely of the national interest. Sadly, to stop the corruption of federal power, many of the programs that need to be shut down or devolved to states, cannot be trusted to many states because they too have become bloated and corrupt. The biblical notion of removing the mote from one's own eye before pointing out another's failures rings true. An added element here is an examination of education and its role in governmental and social disfunction.

Don De Angelo

Part III lays out the case for reforming the federal system. The reality is that only drastic demolition is now possible. Can you "reform" the FBI given what we now know? Is there a justification of perpetuating the powers assumed through the Patriot Act let alone the massive administrative state it created? My previous book tried to be surgical and purposeful. The idea was to move the nation in a more libertarian direction in the hopes that such reforms would lead to an epiphany that small government is a collective good. Recent history has disabused me of my folly.

Part IV lays out possible outcomes should dramatic reforms be rejected. History does not provide clear prophecy of outcomes. However, much of what we are experiencing now have shared themes with other periods and civilizations. It is not meant to scare as much as inform. While I considered not having this part of the work, it has been more evident to me that we all need to accept that, while we are certainly free to choose our path of conduct, we are not free of the consequences of those choices. Current American *progressives* (neo-Marxists) complain about oppressive, systemic abuses but never lay out a specific alternative. As deconstructionists they are more confident in tearing things down than building anything of value. They may also understand that, while many people share their disdain for the modern West, most would shudder to contemplate what modern Marxists have in their minds as the substitute.

There are way too many to thank. My family, while always weary of listening to my diatribes, has always defended my right to speak my mind and supported my attempt to put it all into print. Many mentors: Grandpa August Guenther, all of my aunts and uncles, Coach Wayne Barton, Mrs. McGarvey my high school English teacher, Professor James Magee of the University

The American Revolution

of Delaware, Milton and Marge Ford, parents of a high school friend who insisted that I go back to college and actually came to Parents Weekend to encourage me, Father Michael Carrano, Dr, Richard Kelly, and Joe Kilroy – father figures who kept me on a path of purpose. There are also too many friends over the years who have inspired and encouraged.

I also want to thank Chris Grazier, a colleague who edited my work and gave me encouragement. Larry Broughton is a friend from high school who is now a successful writer, entrepreneur, and public speaker/writer who has been my most recent mentor. Larry has wisdom that never ceases to amaze. Without all these people I am not who I am and there would be no reason to accomplish anything. This work can only be dedicated to all of them.

PART I

Theo-Libertarian Citizenship (TLC)

The American Revolution

In the beginning there was God. This is a rather ominous statement that most people in the West would recognize, even it is not believed. This is because the Bible is the preeminent resource in western literature. After thousands of years, it has started to lose its status in the name of diversity, equity, and inclusion. The problem with this development is that all the rights, privileges, and political culture are founded on biblical principles. The development of this new argument has created a chasm of ignorance among younger Americans, which allows them to disregard the source of some of our most fundamental rights as citizens of the United States. There are also a lot of non-religious Christians and Jews who may act aggressively to defend the Bible but do not embrace the biblical call for civility and tolerance.[8]

A secondary concern is the assumption by more than half of the American public that the government is there to protect us from uncomfortable and or inconvenient realities. This has created a high demand for government services and more importantly government power. For both believers and non-believers this dilemma of wanting more government but insisting on individual freedom is really at the base of our current political disruption. Once you hand over more power to any government in the name of securing one's safety, you are surrendering individual liberties that may never be recovered, at least not without suffering.

The goal for all of us individually and as Americans collectively is to acknowledge our respective roles in creating a civil society.

---

8 Whenever I sense a spiritual idea or theological concept, I am very suspect of my own understanding. This section almost didn't make it in the text. But this video convinced me I was onto something. https://www.youtube.com/watch?v= JOogAC6gHaE.

Don De Angelo

For those Americans who do not subscribe to a religious ethos this means an embrace of what has traditionally been called a civic religion. For those who do embrace a faith-based doctrine this call to render unto Caesar what is Caesar's compels us to be a productive and polite member of society. The "In God we Trust" slogan is reflective of this ideal. Most of our notions of public fairness and ethical behavior are based on religious principles that are centuries old.

The Theo of TLC

Current polls show that an increasingly larger minority of Americans are non-practicing people. This could mean that they are people of faith who simply do not go to church, or they are individuals who have rejected the notion of a specific God or have rejected the idea of the divine entirely. While there are still many Americans who embrace faith practice there is certainly more tolerance for non-believing and the notion that there may be other legitimate faith practices outside of the Judeo-Christian norm.

The problem with this wavering understanding and/or support of Judeo-Christian traditions removes the premise to many of our civil liberties as articulated in the Bill of Rights. A connected issue here is that when a right is no longer attached to a divine or nature centered root it opens a conversation to the possibility of *limited rights*. The result is the rise of individual and institutional discussions on how to curtail what are historically considered fundamental rights simply because they now seem inconvenient or illogical or in some cases an actual threat to democracy itself.

The American Revolution

Related to this is the misplaced anger on the part of traditionalists who understand fully the connection between biblical ideals of right and wrong and what has become the western concept of human rights. It can be very frustrating for those who innately understand these principles and the connections to our freedoms and then be confronted by well-funded sources who seek to either remove that connection or destroy the freedoms in the name of progressive notions of democracy.

Even if one refutes the Christian faith, within the Western tradition is the Enlightenment that has an agnostic perspective that still shares the notion of a universe created by a superior "being". Why does this matter? When studying the American Revolution an essential question is, "Why did our 13 colonies choose to rebel from Great Britain?"

One unique characteristic was that all 13 colonies had two things happening simultaneously. Most American colonists who could read were exposed to the writings of the Enlightenment. John Locke was the most widely read. Virtually all the colonists were Christian and in the 1730s and 1740s a spiritual revival swept every part of British North America. In both these movements came notions of individual sovereignty and liberty. When God created Man, he imparted free will. In this everyone was given the freedom to choose their paths. The suffering of mankind then is a product of imperfect humans acting on that free will and making bad choices.

To give a pathway for Man to be reconciled to God, the law was given to Moses. If Israel obeyed these rules of conduct, God agreed to keep His blessings with the people. High priests would slaughter innocent lambs in sacrifice to the Lord and the nation would remain in His favor. The result was a civil society with a shared political culture. But like all humans, the Israelites chose to not obey the law and instead worshiped other gods or simply stopped demanding Israel follow Adonai.

When the temporal sacrifices proved to be insufficient to cleanse humanity of sin, a "new covenant" was incarnated in Jesus Christ. His death on the cross was the final offering that conquered sin and death. Now mankind could be rid of guilt and shame by simply embracing the *Lamb of God*.

The Great Awakening message was primarily about Protestant/Christian salvation. Colonial religious life was not as regular as one might think. Inside New England, where English Calvinism reigned, many of the younger Puritans were not living up to the normal piety of faith. Many younger members of the community chose not to pursue salvation because the very public nature of the self-examination had become public spectacle and caused many to endure nervous breakdowns. The new generation decided to opt out. In Puritan speak this was essentially choosing to go to hell rather than face possible humiliation. Church elders compromised with *halfway covenants*, which allowed unsaved congregants to stay in the community and have their children baptized, but not have any voting power or say in church governance.

Sermons began to sound dour and mournful. Many preachers shared *jeremiads* of the coming doom if people did not start reviving their commitment to Christ. Not surprisingly, when pandemics and crop failures ensued, people began to engage in self-reflection. Johnathan Edwards gave a two-hour sermon, *Sinners in the Hands of an Angry* God, which was also published. There could be no "half" saved. Those who refused to embark on a journey of salvation were doomed. The allegory was of sinners

The American Revolution

held over the flames like a spider clinging to its last silken string, only to be released into the abyss. The fire was lit and churches all throughout the colonies were challenging conventional thinking within the faith.

One particularly strong subtext of the revival was the notion that each person had a responsibility to seek salvation from the Lord. It was imperative for the individual to determine if one was "called" by God. Faith journeys were collective in practice but at the peril of each soul. This was the idea that we are all created equal and valued. God counts the hairs of our head so we must live as though we matter. We have inherent freedoms, but they come with great responsibility.

To be in this state of Happiness, one must embrace the salvation of Jesus Christ and devote oneself to a life of love and service. The proof of one's grace was a life of success and propriety. Each man in control of himself and his family, growing his own wealth and contributing to the prosperity of the community, is evidence of salvation. From this comes the idea of the protestant work ethic.

The Enlightenment has a similar construct. In the deist narrative, God is a benevolent yet less intrusive Creator. Using the laws of nature, the Creator knit together a universe in which Man emerged dominate due to his ability to reason. When one understands the laws of nature, one knows the mind of God and are therefore enlightened – what many of the philosophes considered a state of Happiness.

Each human being is therefore sovereign of him/herself. In a state of nature Man is entirely good and free. One is good because one is alone and therefore unable to transgress against another, which is the basis of all sin. One is also free because

Don De Angelo

there is no one to impose upon one's ability to live according to one's own reason. This is the primitive state of the innocent. If one is hungry and there is a rabbit, one may pursue the prey and be satisfied. There is not interference and no one to offend.

The dilemma is that few are solitary in life. Humans are social creatures. We enjoy and in fact need the company of fellow human beings to both survive and thrive. Conflict is inevitable because each person's sovereignty now begins to encroach upon another's. When all are hungry and here comes the rabbit, personal wellbeing takes over and the collective experience becomes insufferable. This is a state of chaos; and in such a state everyone's life and liberty are in peril.

Thomas Hobbes writes government is therefore created to bring order out of the chaos. Borrowing from Greek and Roman philosophers who praised the natural trend towards despotic power to control violence; Hobbes felt that only a credible threat of punishment would establish a just society.

John Locke expanded upon this idea of order because he could not believe that order was enough of a value to cause individuals to surrender their sovereignty to potential tyranny. For Locke the submission of the people to any authority was to protect one's rights to life, liberty, and property. The state of Happiness created was the real imperative. But how to ensure that any such subservience would not be abused?

Baron Montesquieu is credited with offering a structural solution. Instead of allowing such governing power to be embodied in one person (a King); authority must be divided among separate entities. Legislatures (parliaments) must draft the laws based on consent of the governed, and the executive then faithfully enforces the will of the people's representatives. The judicial

The American Revolution

interpretation(s) of the law and review of conduct was later added. There was still a risk that even this form of governance would devolve into tyranny.

Jean-Jacques Rousseau is credited with coining the term Social Contract. His final check against tyranny was the right of the people to overthrow any government that failed to use its power to defend and protect the rights of the people. This tacit agreement has existed since time memorial and would always manifest in such a way.

These two ideological expressions are articulated in the Declaration of Independence. When Thomas Jefferson writes of inalienable rights to life, liberty, and pursuit of happiness, he is bowing to both because he knows the colonies will need both adherents to fight England. These values are then imbedded into our political culture. The notion that anyone can appreciate let alone value any rights delineated in such a system without appreciating the sources is foolish.

The problem begins in the 1963 *Vitale v. New York* decision in which the Supreme Court determined that state-sanctioned prayer in public schools was unconstitutional. The opinion was expanded to include any religious expression. The result has been several generations of Americans who have not been exposed to any references to the biblical foundations of the political culture in which we are supposed to live. If there is no acceptable root to rights, then *some* rights can be altered or ignored.

It is not that everyone must be part of the Judeo-Christian faiths to function in a free society. But not understanding the eternal sources of human rights leaves one open to the suggestion that rights come from governments; and this is not only an error of principle but a surrender of sovereign rights. If one

Don De Angelo

can at least intellectually accept the notion that our rights as human beings *preceded* the existence of any government because of some higher intelligence/creation, then the rights of all are best protected.

This fallacy gets used in debates over the Second Amendment. The younger voices begin to argue against the "shall not be infringed" part of the amendment believing that the right existed because of a specific need at a specific time. Society has supposedly *evolved* since then and now the right to bear arms is a threat to internal peace and safety. My jaw drops. That line of logic is very dangerous. Imagine if we were to establish the standard that all our rights had to constantly pass a relevance test. Think about the impact on civil liberties if judges could consider evolutionary changes in social priorities or acceptable conduct.

The permanence that comes from the idea of Nature and Nature's God is paramount to the sanctity of individual freedom. Whether this is accepted in one's heart, head or both will determine the security of these rights. Teaching the Bible is not just a religious exercise. It allows younger Americans a way to understand the foundational support of our essential liberties. It is bad enough that we are no longer assigning the works of the Enlightenment thinkers because they no longer fit the diversity, equity, and inclusion standards of contemporary educators; but excluding any reference to religious contributions to American political culture is a real threat to democracy.

Another unseen or unappreciated value of biblical standards of behavior is that of *self-governance*. Many of the Founding Fathers and/or Framers were not what one might consider devout Christians. Some were either agnostic or deist in their beliefs, if not atheist. But the consensus among them was that some form

The American Revolution

of moral code had to be in place. In a society based on maximum personal liberty there needed to be an uncoerced yet firmly applied sense of responsibility.

John Adams thought that the democratic republic established by the U.S. Constitution was constructed solely for a religious people. Ben Franklin and Thomas Jefferson, two notable non-practicing men, felt that only a people who were trained to curb their own behavior would be able to have a government with limited powers. For example, prohibition may not be an effective way to stop alcoholism; but freedom to drink whatever one wishes will quickly devolve into bacchanalian dystopia without an accepted concepted of temperance, be it tacit or overt.

This is why teaching values to one's children ensures that every generation is well-versed in what is acceptable conduct among most of the society. If I were to move to a Muslim country and wanted to earn a modicum of acceptability, I would be expected to embrace a set of values. I do not have to *believe* the theology that produced the norms, but I should respect it enough to commit myself to complying with those customs.

This is what has caused so many problems with Muslim immigration into Europe. Thousands of refugees were permitted into Europe without first making sure that theses migrants were prepared to embrace the non-Muslim values of the continent. Failure to assimilate has caused distrust and disillusionment. New residents are not accepted because they are practicing *alien* behavior, and the dominant culture is seen as intolerant. Because Europe has been secular for so many generations, there is scant understanding among the majority community as to why there is a problem. This lack of appreciation for the history of where the values come from, allow Europeans to be convinced that it is their culture that is the source of the tension.

For Americans who choose not to adhere to a set of moral values, which in the United States are predominately of Judeo-Christian origin, it feels oppressive to be expected to adhere to social norms that appear to endorse that ideology. Hence the development of sub-cultures that have existed in all societies throughout history. Fortunately, American values include the idea of tolerance, which means anyone can be permitted to live the way one chooses whether one is seen as acceptable. For a very long time this was accommodated in ethnic enclaves and isolated communities – Little Italy and Amish Country, for example.

When a society decides to ignore its historical roots for good conduct, they cease to teach this to their youth. As those children grown, they no longer have a frame of reference for *why* we are called to act in a certain way. Soon the norm as no value attached to it and the assumption becomes holding on to that expectation is not only old fashioned but oppressive or an *obstacle to progress*. Having young people read the *Bible* becomes unacceptable because most citizens have never read it and cannot possibly understand or appreciate its benefits.

There is a danger in the other extreme and it has shown itself in recent history. Many religious Americans have been so engrossed in the current assault on Judeo-Christian values and institutions, that they fail to recall the hostility of faith communities to liberal-minded people and communities. One need not go back too far to find laws and practices that were intentionally punitive of people and conduct deemed *unchristian* by mainstream society.

The personal actions and lifestyles of individuals that violated biblical principles, regardless as to whether that person(s)

The American Revolution

embraced them, was a form of oppression. Using government power to enforce biblical values seems like the holy thing to do; but it requires giving to the government inherently intrusive powers, which it is unlikely to relinquish. Those same powers, when used by that same government under the control of secularists, have wreaked havoc on religious life in the United States. To prevent such a trap society must embrace a more libertarian attitude.

People of Judeo-Christian institutions too often and too quickly forget that their own spiritual fate is not tied up in the religious behavior and choices of others. When we stand before the Creator it is our own actions that will weigh against us. Scripture also informs us that this world is full of unfairness and evil conduct, which is why we are implored to be *in* the world but not *of* the world. Heaven on Earth is possible only in a God-centered reality, and minus that we are stuck with imperfection.

What this means to each of us, regardless of our embrace of faith as important to our personal orientation, we still understand that (A) our rights are based on the concept of a *divine Creator* who imparted these rights **before** there was ever such a thing called government. We also accept that (B) we are expected to use a set of moral principles as a standard of conduct that keeps us *self-regulated* and not a reason for more government control or coercion. For those who do embrace faith, we must remember (C) not to judge those who fail to meet those standards because we all fall short.

Remember, it is always easy to point to the behavior of others and cast blame. The action allows each of us to feel good, even superior. But representative government makes this behavior more suspect. Members of our government are fellow citizens. They serve at the pleasure of the voters. How many of us even know who these people are, let alone take responsibility for how they got into office? Does government grow only because of the natural tendency towards a concentration and expansion of power? It seems that many times, government power grows because we the people prove unable or unwilling to do things for ourselves, hence a demand for more government.

Start with our own personal choices. If I choose to smoke, does society bear any responsibility for the known possible outcomes? Yet, all insurance policies cover for such outcomes, which we all pay. If I cannot control my eating habits and become morbidly obese or diabetic, does the government have the responsibility to help? If I don't pay any attention in school, my parents prefer to blame my teachers, and I fail to obtain the skills to ensure a more secure economic reality for myself; is it really the responsibility of the government or society to make my life more "equal?" These are just a few examples of how our own behavior and the choices we make, create an environment where bigger government becomes a viable option.

Are you living in poverty? What are you really doing to rise above your current reality? Did you graduate high school? This is the number one indicator of whether someone is destined for destitution. Are you trained in any skill? Do you set aside even a little bit of money for a rainy day? Did you take the "free" education you were provided to become as educated as you could and obtain all the skills possible? If you do not have a clear answer to these questions, then your current existence may be more self-inflicted. Are there structural obstacles to rising above poverty? Yes, but most are governmental structures and not market ones. When we challenge ourselves first, we usually find a better

The American Revolution

solution than one imposed by government(s). And the struggle we go through makes us stronger people more capable of facing the next challenges.

Are you more interested in what your child says about you than what that child will contribute to the greater society? If so, then you are a major contributor to the current woes of American life, and a very big reason why there is an ever-intrusive government dictating how supposed adults should parent. Ask any teacher with a difficult child in their classroom. The mystery is usually solved within five minutes of meeting the parents of said problem. Clearing the deck for your child does nothing to build their self-esteem. A trophy for every child may let them feel special now but does nothing to build long-term self-esteem. But it does guarantee that when they are older, they will expect life to be easier than it is. It makes them a burden for society, which usually leads to more government programs to "help," or more coercion to control them. These children will never reach their full potential as human beings, and many will be a pain in our collective butts.

Virtue signaling has also become a major issue. It is easy to call on the government to do things that we feel is good for society because it doesn't require any of us to really do anything except pay more taxes. Whether it is a personal or collective act, doing on our own demonstrates true conviction of purpose. Want to solve the carbon problem, drive less and use public transportation, consume less, and donate to the cause. Put your own money where your supposed conscience resides. If enough people follow suit, then proof of significance is self-evident.

Apps such as Go Fund Me are far better distributors of funds than any government. If you feel someone needs support, then get on the phone and make things happen. We all wait around for the government to act, when in most cases handling the problem on our own is the quickest, most efficient, and most compassionate path. The question we should always be asking is "does this require outside intervention, or are we best capable to do the right thing within our own community?"

Government should be the source of last resort and not the be all and end all collective action(s). If you find yourself discontent with the speed and effectiveness of government then you should understand that the slowness is an inherent characteristic of any government. The effectiveness of government action is more a result of government's divided attention. The federal government has become a *jack-of-all-trades and a master of none*. Not only has it become inept at roles it was never intended to play; but it is increasingly failing at those responsibilities it has the exclusive power to handle. The current crisis at the southern border is one sad example. The result is lower trust in government and a budget increasingly out of control.

Want to know what seems to make a society more compassionate and giving? Actual people reaching out to help their fellow man. Most communities of faith are known to demonstrate a consistent rate of caring and working for positive change. **Reverend** Dr. Martin Luther King, Jr. – I'll say no more. Are you an active person of faith? Your spiritual health is as important as your physical and mental health. It is irrelevant which faith you practice if it is practiced. And don't just start going to services. Be a member of your faith community. There you will discover multiple opportunities to help. Most have outreach to the poor, imprisoned, and homeless. Many places of worship are polling stations during elections and are desperate for volunteers.

The American Revolution

Raising your children in a faith tradition based on caring for one another is a wonderful foundation for their own sense of compassion and self-sacrifice; and the self-regulation that requires less government.

If any positive change is to happen in our government, it must begin with positive changes to our personal and collective behavior. Are you atheist and/or agnostic and feel like you cannot act alone then join any number of social clubs. (You can join even if you are religious). Grab your closest friends who share your desire to make life better and join the Kiwanis, the Elks, Moose, or Eagles fraternities or the Rotary or Lions clubs. These groups are always looking for new members and are dedicated to helping make communities better places to live and work. The fact that no one seems to be joining in to help but calling for "something to be done," is virtue signaling at its worst. Everyone is guilty of this one; but it bears exposing the raw truth that we are often the obstacles to our own solutions.

So, the rule should be (A) we act for ourselves to ensure that we have the best opportunities in life and the most freedom and (B) we share collective burdens with our neighbors to demonstrate compassion and act quickly and more efficiently. (C) When we can't get around the problem we should see if there are private institutions and/or charities who are best positioned to help. When and only when these three steps fail should we be looking to a government to act. Then it should be your local and/or state that should be stepping in first. If you are saying that this is simply not possible any more then, we are truly a society in trouble. If we try all of this and big federal power is the only solution, then we have failed as a civilization.

Don De Angelo

Libertarianism

The word *libertarian* has been thrown around a lot these days. Most unusual is the misuse by self-described liberals and the mainstream media who insist on equate it with right-wing extremism. Ignoring the shared root, liberals contend that any notion that individual rights and minimal government interference are absolute indications of oppressive intent over weaker groups. This is why today's liberals should really be called by their proper, philosophical identity – Marxists. Only a post-modernist, Marxist could corrupt language in such a way to call a person who calls for more personal liberty an oppressor.

What makes the story more complicated and sadder is that many conservatives mistake libertarian with libertine. For those on the right anyone calling for the government to stay out of all human activity involving consenting adults is a license to debauchery. Never mind the libertarian caveat that no such behavior should be permitted when infringing on the rights of others, there is little trust in adults to make proper moral decisions for themselves.

The peril in both misperceptions is the invitation to larger and more intrusive government. If libertarian laws allow all adults to be truly free, the chance that someone might be left out or offended is simply unacceptable to the Marxist and must therefore be brought under government censure. The thought that permitting people to decide how to live their own lives might lead to a rejection of traditional values, which is a worry for those institutions who must convince society of their rightness. No, this is a call for government intervention to force a prescribed code of conduct and a violation of the First Amendment.

The American Revolution

What we are left with is not a right-left spectrum. Both are different forms of big government authoritarianism. While they will fight over which side will exercise the levers of power, they both accept and appreciate the value of that power. Neither group is looking to limit or abolish the wielding of power, but which group will get to use the power to support their agenda or line their own pockets. It should not surprise any of us who have read the philosophes of the Enlightenment. It is human nature to pursue self-interest. If that pursuit involves dispensing with trillions of dollars in other people's money, even more enticing – ALL power corrupts.

My political socialization began with a rather *right-of-center agnosticism*. When I turned 18, I wanted to explore all political ideals and registered as a non-partisan. Over the next ten years there were both Democrat and Republican candidates that seemed worthy of supporting. Even people with whom I did not agree philosophically, I was comfortable voting them into power because they seemed intelligent and reasonable.

In 1992, when I moved to San Diego, I heard a speech by Bill Clinton. There was nothing specific, but his tenor and vibe was off. When a politician says, "I feel your pain" it is based either in empathy or opportunism. Something wasn't right with that guy. In addition, Pat Buchanan was challenging President George H.W. Bush for the Republican nomination. I didn't like him either and, as a student of international relations, I was impressed with how Bush the Elder handled the end of the Cold War and believed he deserved a second term. I registered as a Republican for the first time so that I could participate in the Republican primaries to support the president.

My affiliation with the Republican party seemed the correct one given my right-leaning personal values. But I was not always

Don De Angelo

convicted of the neo-conservative foreign policy and self-righteous preaching on moral behavior. Chasing gay people into the closet with venom and vitriol doesn't seem to make them more likely to embracing the loving salvation of Jesus Christ. The lack of a moral compass in the Clinton administration was the only thing keeping me in the red camp.

The election of 2000 seems to be the beginning of crises for the American republic. The rise of George W. Bush as president and the lawsuits and "not my president" chants of Democrats established a new methodology for political discourse. Only the tragedy of 9/11 saved President Bush's first term. It birthed a new line of conspiracy theories about the deep state and military industrial complex (MIC) in particular. It required, however, the surrender of many of our dearest liberties. By this I am referring to the Patriot Act.

This act of Congress is the singular step that has led to massive transgressions by government against we the people. When the fear tactics used to permit intrusion into all our private lives, I got very nervous. While I was OK with military action to get El Qaida, it was quickly apparent that mission creep was afoot and that our government wanted complete control of Afghanistan. When Bush order the invasion of Iraq, I was looking to abandon ship.

There are plenty of ways to justify some of the decisions made and fears articulated. But when the outcomes produced were excused as *justified* my moral compass began to quiver. There had to be a better answer.

In 2007 I was named a *fellow* of the James Madison Memorial Fellowship Foundation. Even though I had a MA in international relations, this organization gave me a scholarship for a second MA – this one in History – because I was a history and

The American Revolution

government teacher in California. A total of 60 such teachers for across the United States and some from foreign countries were given this honor. The experience unintentionally exposed me to the ideals of libertarianism; and at 43 years of age, it changed my political orientation. As part of my studies, I attended a summer seminar sponsored by the foundation at Georgetown University. It encompassed two graduate courses on the history of the U.S. Constitution. That's when I was introduced to James Madison.

Now I knew all the basic facts of Madison and thought he was a cool guy. Let's face it, no matter how short you are, being the "Father of the Constitution" and the author of the U.S. Bill of Rights makes you a big man on campus. For the first time, I had to *study* the Constitution and the entire notes Madison had taken at the Constitutional Convention. I also read the entire *Federalist Papers* and the counter arguments in the *Anti-Federalist* articles. It was the very first time I had ever read the antifederalist works.

For those who teach American government classes to high school seniors, there may not be an immediate problem. All textbooks mention the Antifederalist party and their opposition to ratifying the constitution. There are however two issues of concern.

First, the antifederalist position is in many ways the libertarian view of a democratic republic. Decentralization of power, limited areas of government control, and the sanctity of individual liberty all point in the libertarian direction. Most Marxist narratives of constitutional history imply that because the U.S. Constitution was ratified, the antifederalist/libertarian argument was invalidated – for good. Those politicians who continued to

40

Don De Angelo

push for such ideals were not just flawed in their politics, but a threat to the Union.

This gets credence because many of the antifederalists, who were extensively in the southern Democrat party, were supporters of slavery. Using the antifederalist argument that most powers were *reserved* to the states, these Democrats posited that their stance on human chattel was none of the nation's business. The ensuing Civil War was the natural outcome and a national *Iliad*. Anti-federalism (and by extension libertarianism) was now linked to support for slavery and treason.

For the next fifty years it was seen as the federal government's right, if not purpose, to be the objective umpire of the Union. The advent of Populist and then Progressive agendas gave impetus to expanded federal power into areas long considered the prerogative of the states if any government at all. It was this era when Marxist theory got its foothold in American academia and began to infiltrate liberal political agendas.

The inevitable expense and errors of big government gave rise to a new resistance to federal power. It was now the Republican party, which resisted and this time it was for the protection of corporate and industrial interests. The liberal economics of the Enlightenment found its champion in the party that approved big tariffs, cheap labor, and American industrial hegemony. For the next decades the two parties essentially fought over these two priorities – small government in favor of economic power, or big government to protect the worker from the callous greed of corporate profit motives.

The Great Depression and World War II gave living credence to the idea of an aggressive federal power. It is interesting to note that centralized authority and intrusiveness of government is less

The American Revolution

feared in times of national crisis. When considering that in 1932 most Americans had a living memory of World War I, the Spanish Flu pandemic, and the stock market crash of 1929. What you have is a population primed for big government with little restraint. By 1945 you have a nation that withstood considerable disasters and emerged as the world's industrial superpower.

The Cold War only made big government seem more tolerable. In this we see a "post-war" consensus, wherein Democrats and Republicans essentially embraced Keynesian economics in domestic policy and containment regarding the Soviet Union and foreign policy. This was the beginning of the blurring of the two parties.

The collapse of the Soviet Union in 1991 did usher in a less-convivial discourse between the parties. But while the partisanship drew sharp rhetoric among voters, the politicians themselves seem to have focused the bulk of their attention on maintaining the consolidated power of the federal government. This was originally a discussion of what to do with the *peace dividend;* and to their credit, the parties were able to balance the budget and provide for a potential two trillion-dollar surplus. Had all gone according to plan, by 2010 the U.S. debt would have been less than $4 trillion.

The terrorist attacks of 2001 changed all of that. Like the attacks on Pearl Harbor in 1941, the 9/11 tragedy was a turning point in America's post-Cold War euphoria. There are many possible theories as to why the U.S. was struck and what were the most viable options for retaliation. But what is singularly clear is that it ushered in a new era of big government. A new fear gave many citizens the excuse to surrender liberties. The Patriot Act was the result, and it created a codified intrusion into the private

Don De Angelo

lives of all Americans. It also established the excuse for a litany of wars of choice. It may have diminished terror attacks on the homeland, which is impossible to measure in part because we are denied access to documentation in an overly classified body of data; but it certainly unleashed surveillance industrial complex (as newly coined by the "Twitter Files") and destabilized and already dystopic Middle East.

The Libertarian party was founded in 1971. Libertarians "strongly oppose any government interference into their personal, family and business decisions." Embracing the non-aggression principle that violence must never be used to promote ideology, the party believes that "all Americans should be free to live their lives and pursue their interests as they see fit as long as they do no harm to another."[9]

For this system to function requires the government to be extremely small and for citizens to police themselves. It is magnificent in concept, but one might argue impossible in practice unless the above explained *Theo-Libertarian Citizenship* (TLC) is also embraced. It becomes a dilemma because we must ask everyone to understand theological foundations to our collective political culture, while also expressing and acting in tolerance for those who choose not to embrace those values.

A comparison would be teaching English literature without Shakespeare or the King James version of the *Bible*. One need not embrace the theology, but the impact of both on the language is undeniable and must be understood otherwise one concludes that it has no value at all or that English is just some random evolution of words. Many schools have stopped teaching either

---

9   https://www.lp.org/about/

The American Revolution

because they are seen as too white (Shakespeare) or too oppressive (biblical literature).

What libertarianism offers is a standard of conduct in the public sphere. We can all understand collective political culture while tolerating deviance so long as it does not impinge on the rights of others. Libertarian philosophy also places fundamental value on individual liberty, which offers protection to any minority against forms of oppression and tyranny. Begin by making the Bill of Rights truly *uninfringed*. Then use strict construction when applying the Tenth Amendment and loose construction when applying the Ninth Amendment. The result is a central government that perpetually kept in check and individual liberty as a permanent requirement of national institutions.

The more one studies the ideals the more one sees the expression of the Founding Fathers in general and the Framers more specifically. Congress functions on the democratic value of majority rule, but the Bill of Rights and the practice of filibuster and checks and balances are libertarian tools to defend the rights of those who might dissent.

Another example is taxation, which was a main reason for our separation from England. A libertarian would say, "all taxation is theft." A typical response might be that of Oliver Wendell Holmes, Jr in that "taxes are the price we pay for civilization." But this assumes that the people are incapable of being civil without the coercive hand of government.

Libertarians would argue that if anyone has the power to approve a tax, they must do so with the understanding that the revenue collected is not *the government's money*. It belongs to those citizens from whom it was taken by some degree of force. To assume otherwise is to see the right to pursue happiness as

Don De Angelo

something under government control and not inalienable – granted by *Nature and Nature's God.*

It is inevitable that power will become corrupt, so keeping government small (not letting government interfere in most parts of human affairs) is the only way to protect against tyranny. The push to cut taxes becomes the last attempt at keeping government from becoming *Leviathan* and uncontrolled. When Marxist cry that this is starving government what they really mean is killing power.

The libertarian means of limiting government power is to devolve it as close to the individual as possible. As will be discussed later, federalism was the proscribed system to check centralized power. The U.S. Senate was key to that control, but that was ended with the 17th Amendment. The only reason for the Senate to exist was to give the states a national mechanism to stop the unfettered growth of federal power. Changing that construct and giving the Senate seats over to democratic appeal erased any remanence of state sovereignty. The federal system would only function properly was if everyone remained committed to the original plan.

Citizenship in a Free Country

So far, we have looked at how each person contributes to liberty by self-regulation with the use of a moral code that has been agreed upon by most of the society as a desired behavioral outcome. This must be coupled with a charitable heart which can tolerate those who dissent so long as there is respect for the majority opinion. When citizens embrace this lifestyle there is a

The American Revolution

civil society, which requires minimal coercion. In such a reality the demand for government force is low.

One of the praises of American democracy by Alexis de Tocqueville was that American religiosity and free associations created a self-reliant society with little need for governance. It was not that there were no bad people, but that communities dealt with them locally based on shared values. This made national politics less important in the sense that central decisions had less impact on local and personal happiness. The national government therefore had fewer areas of control and fewer decisions to make. What little power the federal government had was more easily mastered and less likely to be corrupted.

Next, we look at collective realities that must come in any society. The stability of community demands popular participation. Voluntary associations are at the heart of a libertarian vision of social order. Most of the day-to-day issues should be solely handled by locals building consensus among themselves without state or federal interference. Here is where we all have lost our way. Remember Welcome Wagons? They were people in the neighborhood set up teams to go and introduce themselves to people who have just moved in and might need information on how to get certain things done, or on local schools, or recreation options. What happened to block parties and co-ordinated Halloween *trick-or-treat* events? It starts with little things like this.

It is at the heart of socio-political reform. What is required to make a new idea work? We see this at every level. If your company embarks on a new business model (assuming most employees have had a say in its actualization) and someone chooses to resist those changes, the concept may never get a fair chance to

Don De Angelo

succeed. When a family needs to rethink its finances, and takes up a new spending behavior, hidden credit cards are a landmine waiting to destroy everything. If you are hanging out with friends trying to decide on that evening's event and no one can settle on one enjoyable thing that everyone wants to do, the whole night is ruined.

When examining the current U.S. situation and possible remedies, it is good to remember the observation of Pogo: "I have met the enemy, and he is us!"[10] It becomes vital to remember that we each have a role to play. Anyone who thinks that Donald Trump created the acrimony exhibited in American politics has simply not been awake the last fifty years. Show young people today video of the Democratic National Convention in 1968 and watch their reaction to the anger, hostility, and violence. We haven't seen that at a convention since – thank goodness – but that year could be viewed as the real catalyst of our current, collective angst.

The first expectation is to follow the laws without the need of supervision. In other words – be an adult! Go into any downtown on a weekend evening and literally count those who fail in this area alone. No need to be a prude. But too many of us drive when drunk, fight in public, and speed excessively. All these actions cause the remaining community to fear enough for their own safety to call on the government to act. This becomes the rationale for bigger political enterprise. That truth should give all of us pause. John Adams observed that

---

10   In 1971, Walt Kelly did a cartoon to support the new Earth Day. It was a play on a quote from the War of 1812 when a navy captain reported "We have met the enemy and they are ours."

The American Revolution

the constitutional government established in 1787 was written solely for a religious people because only such a population would be capable of self-awareness and self-regulation. Otherwise, the inevitable breakdown of social order would lead to demand for a strong central power able and willing to impose order, Thomas Hobbes had posited was the essential purpose of all government.

Expand this analysis into the political. More that 40% of American adults fail to vote. That number increases significantly for primary elections, local office contests, and referendum votes. How many do not show up for jury duty? There used to be a common slogan in American political discourse: "If you don't vote, don't bitch!" Now, social media allows anyone to feel entitled to share their opinion without having the obligation to act.

If you feel that the two parties are simply a "duopoly of power," then you share an opinion with millions of your fellow citizens. That is not a reason to become politically inert. It has become a more common observation today to hear a person say they hate the two-party system; but rather than vote for a third party they simply stay home.

The remedy is to register as a member of the party that most closely represents your political sentiments. You must then vote for candidates of that party regardless of possible outcomes. If all of us voted our consciences, we might just be amazed to see how much we are not alone in our feelings. Don't vote for the lesser of two evils. Choose people who best reflect your views. If the Democrats and Republicans begin to see rising support for third parties, they will be forced to listen to new ideas even if they remain in the majority.

Don De Angelo

Most third parties in American history have been single issue parties – Liberty Party (end to slavery); Prohibition Party (end to enjoying life – kidding) – they became very big vote-getters. The reason they disappeared is because one or both main parties adopted their issue into their own platforms. The Republican party was created in 1854 by a coalition of third parties based primarily on federalist priorities of support for a national bank, internal improvements to connect the West to East Coast markets, and the end to slavery.

Philosophical third parties espouse a different way of viewing the role of government. The Libertarian party is in this category. The party sees the role of the federal government as a small and limited one. Most power should be exercised at the state and local level. In fact, most Libertarians believe that MOST decisions should be made by individuals and the communities in which they live. The Green party has the opposite view but also sees a flaw in the American political system. Based on a Marxist worldview, it wants the federal government, primarily, to be the agent of equal outcomes. Everyone should be afforded a basic level of comfort, regardless of their own behavior.

Democrats and Republicans have traditionally been the two-sides of one political spectrum. Democrats have been for more centralized authority with a large welfare state, while Republicans have supported state power and lower taxation. The current manifestations of both parties demonstrate a polarization towards the more extreme positions. Democrats are now a party of socialism, and the Republicans are now the party of military-nationalism. If we don't like this extremism, then our only option is to look for alternative parties.

The American Revolution

It may very well be that, were the American middle to vote for third parties, the traditional main parties would indeed reform. It would not be ahistorical. Forcing the two parties to adopt other opinions or priorities into their own platforms is still reforming the system. But, unless voters demonstrate a willingness to abandon the duopoly, there is no current pressure for either to change. Three decades of failed fiscal policy and a ridiculous national debt surpassing $30 trillion should suffice the condemnation of both parties. The inability of the GOP to settle on one person for the speakership in 2023 garners little confidence in the conservative's ability to govern effectively.

This is particularly true for younger adults. While college students and their peers may feel, they have fresh and creative ideas about how the government should act, few bother to vote. The outcome has been a serious abuse of power that directly impacts younger Americans and tells current politicians that they may ignore the protestations of young people without fear of political damage.

Example. In the late 1970s there was an epidemic of drunk driving fatalities. Most of the victims and perpetrators were young people. Mothers Against Drunk Driving (MADD) formed to impel the federal government to deal with the issue. Members of MADD felt that the states were too inconsistent with their drinking and driving laws. When Ronald Reagan became president, MADD began a push at the national level. It was a genuine and pressing issue. Moms might be an eclectic group, but they share one thing in common – they vote! Moms are a very reliable voting bloc. Only the elderly vote in higher percentages.

President Reagan had a dilemma. He wanted to show moms that he cared deeply about a real and terrible problem; but had to remain a man of small government. The decision was made to insert a section in a highway bill. Any state that did not raise their drinking age to 21 would no longer qualify for federal highway money. This was political genius because Reagan was able to support MADD without establishing a new federal agency to regulate states. He won over millions of female voters without having to fear the backlash of younger voters, who quite frankly weren't even motivated enough to know the workings of the law, let alone bother to vote to reverse it.

Additionally, it would be an interesting "what-if" to think about whether the current national debt would be this high if younger voter were to have a larger percentage of participation? It seems hard to imagine that the two parties would be as loose with spending were younger voters aware of the implications to their future tax burden. The debt keeps rising because older Americans who do vote are running up a tab, they know they will never have to pay. Since the younger generation doesn't vote in any consistent or reliable way, *they* will pay!

Anyone under the age of 30 was born and raised after the end of the "post-war consensus" that followed World War II until the end of the Cold War. You have grown up watching the two-party system devolve into acrimony and confusion. You were raised primarily by Baby Boomers who are, as a generation, selfish and self-absorbed. Your tendency to go ballistic online but *feel threatened* in real life reflects an upbringing that gave ribbons to everyone and trophies to every player. You have seen people come unglued because of something said to them and have become yourselves afraid of words.

All of this has created an environment where political correctness is portrayed as "safe spaces" and speech sensitivity. Your

The American Revolution

generation has an opportunity to demonstrate the spirit of our Founders by rejecting the false narrative of acrimony and fear and embracing the fight for freedom.

The younger generations are the most creative, most informed, and most internationally connected of all human history. Your potential to solve multiple vexing problems and preserve individual liberty is limitless. You can take the technology that your generation has mastered and create a world where everyone is permitted into the conversations and government need not interfere. Utopianism should not be the goal, but a better existence is within your reach.

The difficulty of adjusting to real life after "growing up" and the embrace of Donald Trump by the Republican party has made your generation look long and hard at socialism. Recent polling shows an increasing appeal of socialist ideals than any previous generation.[11] It is interesting to notice that many of these same young people are not as savvy about what exactly socialism means or how it has played out historically.[12] The silly reality is that most students do not make the connection between socialism and Marxism or communism. Most young people are living a life of comfort unknown to most of humanity, ever. The lack of any personal connection to abject poverty makes them vulnerable to the "equity" mantra of progressive ideology. It is easy to support the possibility of fairness when you are uninformed about the historical reality of the policy, which is the

---

11   https://www.axios.com/exclusive-poll-young-americans-embracing-social ism-b051907a-87a8-4f61-9e6e-0db75f7edc4a.html.

12   Soave, Robby, "Socialism is Back, and the Kids are Loving It'" *Reason*. Volume 51, Number 4, August/September, 2019. Pp.52-55.

Don De Angelo

impoverishing of entire societies. Would young people vote for such policies if it meant that most people would face starvation?

Part of this stems from the false-choice narrative projected by most media outlets. The pounding away at Trump's rhetoric, and the complete exclusion of other alternative voices, creates the impression that one must either embrace a populist demagogue or turn to an ideology that will destroy our own political culture. Just because one finds Trump repulsive should not mean rejection of the Enlightenment ideals that created our nation. It is amazing that an entire (media) industry, created by the founding ideals of free speech and free press, would try to manipulate people (especially the young) into making such a stark choice. Fortunately, young people are as committed to freedom and value their own personal economy enough that such a fate will not befall this country.

It is what Bernie Sanders and Alexandria Ocasio-Cortez do not say about socialism that is most important. The most-false claim is that all of Europe operates under "democratic socialism." The best one could say is that most of Europe have very big welfare states. But this is not socialism. There is no minimum wage in Sweden, for example.[13] The reason being is that pure socialism cannot and never has produced a strong enough economy to afford the welfare programs that the American Marxists are so quick to praise. The current Marxist systems operating today – China, Cuba, North Korea, and Venezuela -- all depend on capitalist economies to exist. This is why these regimes get so hostile whenever they are excluded from international economic

---

13   https://www.youtube.com/watch?v=MerkGUx-2V4 This site has an excellent discussion about the Scandinavian "socialist" reality.

The American Revolution

exchanges and use their bad behavior as a form of extortion against the West to gain better trade agreements and/or capital infusions.

Secondly, it is important to realize that many of Europe's populations are backing away from their full support of such programs. Since the end of the Cold War, America's willingness to underwrite the full cost of defending Europe, many governments have had to face the *guns-versus-butter* dilemma that has placed pressure on U.S. policymakers. The Danes for instance privatized their social security system because it is simply too costly in the long run. Financial analysis places the Danish free market retirement plan higher in secure rankings. The English healthcare system is constantly in need of additional funds and proper resources.

Society has only two mechanisms to make a socialist program work – increase revenue and/or control cost. Again, liberal economic theory (capitalism) is the answer to a socialist problem. This means that whenever the government takes over any public good, it must have a constant stream of money and the ability to control who obtains the benefits of such goods and which goods are distributed.

We tend to applaud universal health care in other nations because it seems like such an easy response to our perceived crisis. If you travel to Europe and have a medical issue, you might marvel at the "free" attention you were given. But none of it is free.

As an example, Europeans do not have the luxury of having Tommy John surgery to repair a pitcher's throwing arm. To a government-run system there is simply zero priority for such and expense. Unless you have the private funding for such a procedure, which means perhaps coming to the U.S., then you simply must live with the fact that your dream of playing in the MLB is now over. The data on waiting times, even for important medical problems, is longer than most Americans would ever tolerate. And it's not free -- the taxes are very high.

The Democratic party is currently debating whether to allow private insurance along with their promised "Medicare for all." But what that means is that we will eventually have the exact system we have today. Inadequate, and inconsistent healthcare for the poor and awesome concierge-like service for the wealthy. The only difference is that all of this will add trillions of dollars to the national debt.

The promised "free" education promised by the Left is another canard meant to lure younger voters into the Marxist camp. But consider the facts. In Europe's beloved free college there are multiple mechanisms to limit who gets to go to college. In Germany and other states, exams are given to students at a very young age to determine which children will have the best chance of success at university. If the pupil fails, these they are placed in non-university curriculums that means they will either be given vocational training or job placement assistance prior to graduating high school.

The university life in Europe is nothing like that in the United States. There are no college sports conferences, no student health and fitness centers, and often no extra-curricular programs at all. Most are no-frills, straight forward educational facilities. Professors are unionized government employees who have no incentive to make certain that you graduate. If fact, weeding out the weak is part of the cost-saving aspect of the system.

And again, everyone pays for this "free" education with their taxes. So, if you never qualify to go to college, you will still pay

The American Revolution

for others to go, and they are destined to make more money than you. How is that for "fairness?" If you are lucky enough to graduate from your "free" college, you will pay even higher taxes for the rest of your life. At least with college loans there is a "pay-off" date. The projected trillions of national debts have no end date in site.

It is always good to keep one thing in mind. As a free people, we can choose how we want to order our lives. The United States could realize the dreams of the Marxist wing of the American political spectrum. But it will never erase all the problems and it would require an authoritarian government. Karl Marx was a Utopian writer, but his ideology has created no Eden. If we want to go in this direction, we must understand that we must tolerate massive taxation (at east 50% for most Americans and even more for wealthier people) and have significantly fewer choices on how to live our lives. We also risk the ruination of what is left of our current, vibrant economy, which will never exist in a Marxist system. It is perfectly acceptable to decide to live under a completely different political ideology. The desire of such radical change should only happen in an environment of free and open debate with a fully informed electorate. To attempt restructuring society under the delusion that it can be done at no cost to individual freedom or social cohesion is irresponsible and probably suicidal.

PART 2
The Bear Flag Republic

The American Revolution

Introduction

In the original framework of our federal system, the states were meant to exercise the most power. There is a reason for the 50 separate states in our Union. Most of the founding fathers, especially the Framers, believed a republic that was too large or held too many people would eventually collapse. The Roman Empire began as a city-state, a republic whose economic and political system grew prosperous and powerful. The military system created to protect commerce and trade became the envy of the ancient world. Over time many other states called upon the Romans to help them deal with pesky neighbors or expand trade and the Romans eventually incorporated these states into their massive imperium.

The result was a massive empire engulfing hundreds of ethnicities and languages and covering thousands of square miles. The pressure to centralize authority to deal with the complex administration was too much, which lead to the Roman imperial system most of us acknowledge today. Too big to fail? Too bad!

The focus was on what I refer to as the ***SHEW – social, health, education, and welfare*** policies. For the first hundred years under the Constitution, these issues were exclusively the realm of private, mostly religious organizations. There seems to have been two factors that changed this. First, as the nation became more urban and industrial, the scale of reforming society seemed more ominous. Secondly, the Second Great Awakening of the early 19th Century created a belief that *"I am my Brother's Keeper."* Once the task of reforming society was seen as both imperative and overwhelming, the natural tendency was to look for an *objective* outside actor to impose change. Marxist ideology had

Don De Angelo

been circulating in academic circles for decades by then and the Populist Party and the Progressives tried to mix all of these into a political platform that is referred to today as the *liberal* agenda.

At first these experiments in *government-as-umpire* were done at the state level. Had nothing else extraordinary happened this may have been the norm for the country. But history is not static and events of the early 20th Century terrified enough Americans to demand a federal response to human suffering. As stated earlier, the expansion of federal power began with the world wars and economic depression and then expanded into The Great Society programs of Lyndon Johnson, where the SHEW shifted permanently into federal programs in which the states are told what to do in exchange to federal cash.

Richard Nixon was the first president to challenge this paradigm with his New Federalism proposal, which was simply a call to devolve such powers back to the states. The notion is it would liberate the creative ideation of state and local government to address SHEW issues without requiring amending the Constitution or repealing the 17th Amendment. This became part of the Red/Blue debate over the role of the federal government. While the debates happened, the federal bureaucracies continued to grow both in size and power. The public employee unions found that they could contribute to mostly Democrat campaigns, both in money and volunteers, and have direct influence in direction of US policies and in their own financial advancement.

This is the real creation of the *deep state* in the sense of a self-perpetuating and mostly unaccountable government entity. By the time Donald Trump decided to run for the White House in 2016, there was a sizable electorate that was convinced of its existence and resented its elitist approach towards the people. It

The American Revolution

was the realization that *public servants* not only lived better lives than those they served but also the abundant examples showing a contempt for the people they served.

The *Resistance* to President Trump was entirely perpetuated by the federal bureaucracy and the Democrat Party that depends so much on it for its political and financial success. The revelation that several Republicans were also more comfortable in the arms of the state than in the state on their constituents only confirmed the depth of the problem. The entire saga of the impeachments of Donald Trump were based on a set of stories designed, disseminated and judicated by the deep state. As his persecutions increase so does his popularity. It underscores the breadth of resentment for the elitist and undemocratic behavior of the duopoly that is the deep state.

No other state in the Union exemplifies the failure of big government more than California. An economy that ranks larger than most countries has not prevented the Golden State from taking itself to near fiscal collapse. Under Governor Gavin Newsom, the only imperative of the state was to be the beacon of *resistance* to Donald Trump and MAGA Republicans. The current government posits that the main problem is a lack of new programs. The few Republicans left in the state try to make their presence known and stop tax increases, but they lack the political numbers in either chamber of the legislature (Assembly or Senate) to make any real waves, resulting in a dysfunctional state government and a stagnated economy.

As a California resident for 30 years, I had a vested interest in the outcome of any future changes. Like the debate going on at the national level, the state of California faces a similar fork in the road – either give more power to the government or shrink the size of Sacramento in favor of local regimes, or better yet private enterprise.

California Democrats contend that revenues have not kept pace with the growing demand for state services, focusing on the taxes associated with Proposition 13 a ballot measure from the 1970s initiated because the growing popularity of living in California was driving up property values, and therefore taxes. Older citizens living on a fixed income found they may have paid off their mortgages, but they now faced eviction because of the constantly rising property taxes on their increasingly valuable homes. Proposition 13 restricts the state from reassessing property values until the property changes hands.

Arthur Laffer studied Proposition 13 to demonstrate his theory of taxation – known as the Laffer Curve.[14] Laffer's study demonstrated that the lowered tax rates were spurring more real estate sales that in turn increased revenues to the state's treasury. The lower property taxes also encouraged more people to move to the state, which increased both income and sales tax collection. The real problem for California rests in creating new and expansive programs without the proper budgetary constraint to ensure long-term viability.

What makes California's troubles more entrenched is the causes are structural in nature, as opposed to the mere constitution-interpretation issues discussed under the federal government. California has been operating under a populist political system based on direct democracy mechanism begun during the

---

14　Arthur Laffer's main thesis is that as tax rates go down it encourages more economic activity, which leads to additional revenue to the treasury. Ronald Reagan later named Laffer Chairman of the Council of Economic Advisors.

The American Revolution

Progressive Era. The referendum, initiative, and recall devices, which were started to promote more open government, have become a way for political insiders to force the legislature to adopt new spending obligations without having to worry about the fiscal ramifications. The state constitution is where the reform must start and may require a completely new constitutional convention.

This is intimidating. The variety of political thought in California would create a chaotic convention. Neo-Marxist activism on campuses have distorted the concept of democracy as a desired end unto itself, rather than reinforcing the value of a democratic republic, which is the constitutionally mandated system. Unless a clear majority of strict constructionists were elected as drafters, the new constitution might come out even more convoluted and cumbersome.

The priority is to eliminate these offending budget busters. The mere fact the state would not be holding special elections every year would save the state millions. The next order of business would be to dissolve the several hundred special commissions appointed to govern every aspect of a Californian's life. If any cause requires the state's attention, legislative committees can address these issues.

Restructuring the legislature to reflect the national constitution is necessary and beneficial. Expanding the size of the state assembly to reflect the larger population and adjusting the state Senate so each county council appoints a senator, perhaps in staggered elections, would ensure Sacramento would not use the local governments to pay for non-funded state tasks, thus saving the state millions in election costs.

Embracing federalism, the state can focus on its main priorities. While any libertarian would want to see the SHEW taken

Don De Angelo

over by private/religious entities at the local level, the counties could focus their efforts on these day-to-day issues. By dividing the responsibilities, Californians, and just about all states, would benefit from accountable, responsive government at a lower cost.

Without a solid plan now, California will wallow in a financial morass. Nothing proposed in this book is meant to be gospel. The purpose of this work is to get a conversation started on possible alternatives to the current pattern of conduct in California's government and the problems created by a single-party (Democrat) domination and virtual non-existent (Republican) opposition.

California as a Case Study

"We're the fifth largest economy in the world!"[15] -- has become the fallback statement whenever anyone dares to question the powers that run California. Fiscal apologists throw around the comment so much it borders on cliché, effectively ending discussion rather than enhancing it. Somehow the fact that California has so much economic power means any action done by its government must, by default, be the right thing. However, California suffers from many systemic defects that make the *Golden State* more of a *Gilded State*. Socialist agendas also obligate state citizens to make massive contributions to the treasury. More not-so-hidden liabilities bode ill for the future. The

---

15 https://www.businessinsider.com/california-economy-ranks-5th-in-the-world-beating-the-uk-2018-5

The American Revolution

combination makes for a chilling read. To ignore them risks drowning in denial river!

California teeters on the brink of being too big. While it is too big to be compared to other states, California may be too small to be a real country. Socialists who feared that Donald Trump would drag the nation into a capitalist, dystopian nightmare where no one has health care and the people are forced to sell organs to pay their rent, started the "Calexit" idea as part of a greater *resistance* movement. The irony that "Blue" California would resort to anti-federalist notions of nullification of federal law, especially in areas of immigration and drug enforcement, belies the idea that this is a movement based on integrity and ideological purity. Rather than pursue a constructive alternative to Republican policies, the radical element of the Democratic party has instead made California the test lab for democratic socialism.

The fear and loathing may make for good political rhetoric, but it also allows Californians to defer any conversation about what is structurally wrong with our own state. The fact we are just one state in a large nation keeps us in a mental rut, unable to fathom any other structure that might solve our problems. The discussion boils down to just two options: (A) California becomes an experiment in democratic socialism; or (B) California separates into anywhere from two to six states.

There is another alternative. Using the U.S. Constitution as a guide, why not restructure the state of California in the manner of federalism? Why not consider a state government with complete, but limited powers, and county and city governments given the remaining authority?

Don De Angelo

The State's Authority

The power in Sacramento should be absolute when it comes to certain issues, while leaving other decisions to be handled at the county and local levels. By limiting the state's direct involvement, room exists for both innovation at the community level and cost control of burgeoning bureaucratic systems. If the state limits its powers to a handful of functions it can perfect its exercise of power, which gives voters more confidence in the state's ability to help.

In Sacramento a Department of Justice should run the state courts and regulate prosecutions. The Department of Higher Education would oversee the University of California and California State university systems. The state government also would maintain standards for admissions into these institutions, thus guiding curriculum for pre-K through community college education. The preferred way would be through entrance requirements for the UC and CSU systems. The day-to-day operations of pre-K through high schools should be left to the counties.

The Department of the State would administer all interior state issues, including hiring and firing of state employees and reporting actions of the state government to its citizens and the federal government. The Department of the Interior would handle all infrastructure, including transportation, communication, water access, and environmental regulation.

Sacramento would be best served to exit the "state promotion" business. Private entities always do it better and cheaper. If state entities do their jobs properly, then the state will sell itself. If various industries want to "sell" California, they will spend the money unless they can convince the state to do it for them. The state of

The American Revolution

California is simply too large to know industries and the counties/cities that need promoting. To sustain a permanent bureaucracy to complete such a task misappropriates tax-payer money, which perpetuates the very corporate welfare that needs eliminating.

County Jurisdiction

Every state is different. In smaller jurisdictions one government structure serves the citizenry best by preventing duplication. Smaller bureaucracies are better. Reformers must realize that public employees are hard-working, dedicated professionals, who are committed to help. Yet, the problem is two-fold. First, there are simply many functions the private sector performs better. For example, there is no reason to maintain a state workforce for road repair when private paving companies will do it better and frees the state from paying expensive benefits. Secondly, technology creates abilities that should eliminate thousands of workers within the bureaucracy. While no one should be happy to see people lose their jobs, let alone careers, the truth is we are sustaining workers on the payroll who are simply not necessary. No one who is already registered as a lawful driver in the state should ever have to go into a DMV again. The time has come to replace workers with technology, a reality impacting every sector of the economy, except government.

With that said, the local level is the best place to locate "big" government, in the sense of operating the SHEW. If California were the size of say, New Mexico, it would be more appropriate to assign these tasks to municipalities or cities. By placing many responsibilities at the county level, we create more responsive government while limiting diversity of process to just the 58 counties. The beauty of this structure is San Francisco County could essentially have a socialist system operating if that is what the people there chose, so long as San Franciscans pay for it.

Counties should deal with those everyday issues many citizens confront. An easy solution is to simply name them the Commissions of Public whatever. The Commission on Public Safety would include police, sheriff, fire, and EMT services. For example, the Commission on Public Education would include pre-K, elementary, junior, and senior high schools, and vocational and community college institutions. The Commission on Public Transportation would orchestrate bus and rail networks. The Commission on Public Health could provide single-payer insurance for short and long-term disability, as well as catastrophic insurance paid by a separate tax on all citizens. The Commission on Public Sanitation would deal with water purification, sewerage, and waste collection/storage. The Commission on Public Parks and Recreation would monitor all public spaces.

The imperative in all of this is to bring most daily public services into the administrative hands of locally elected officials. The state maintains unquestioned authority over those functions that require statewide coordination and cooperation. The reforms are also directed at minimizing the size of expensive bureaucracies and wasteful commissions that seem more inclined to promote cronyism than serve the public good.

Cities

In a state the size of California reformers must be tempted to give most of the powers to local governments. And yet, the cities

The American Revolution

of this state impact a much wider area outside traditional city boundaries. Therefore, leaders should incorporate most powers within county governments to ensure everyone impacted by urban activity get a say in how those cities operate. Historically, some city governments dictate behavior to their surrounding communities. As a result, the best function for cities in this structure is to have them elect a mayor who would sit on a "chamber of commerce" board to promote the city in the cultural, business, and tourism sectors. As will be demonstrated later, mayors would also have a county legislative role.

The State Functions

With limited powers, the state government can focus on a handful of items needing statewide coordination. The purpose of restricting state action is to promote better outcomes. Bucking the adage *Jack of all trades but a master of none*, taking several responsibilities off the state government's to-do list creates an opportunity for the state to excel at those few areas in its control. A bicameral legislature helps to stabilize this structure for any such state.

Representation

The state of California boasts nearly 40 million people in an incredibly diverse breakdown. There are several geological and social realities one will not find in most states. The idea 80 assembly persons can represent adequately such a large and varied population is not supportable. To make the state government more responsive to its people would require 175 Assembly members.

The California Assembly is a professional legislature meaning the representatives work year-round and are paid accordingly. In the meantime, the state tasks over 300 commissions with regulating the various elements of state life. These commissions should be abolished and replaced with Assembly Committees to oversee the work of the Departments listed above. Having more legislators to breakdown these tasks is more than adequate to get the job done and to remove the commissions, which have become a repository of political cronyism and wasteful spending. If the state government does not operate properly, citizens can un-elect culpable persons. Commissions are unaccountable to the people and contribute to the slow pace of progress.

The California Senate, which should represent the county governments should comprise 58 senators. The preferred method would entail allowing the county governments to appoint a representative to the state legislature's upper chamber. The Senate would operate best to simply take all legislation proposed by the assembly and respond with one of three options: Amend; Approve; Reject. The Senate would primarily ensure the state government was not trying to creep its way back into issues and/or powers that have been delegated to the counties and/or cities. This set-up promotes a more fluid legislative process: (A) ALL bills would originate in the State Assembly; (B) The Senate would review all bills for errors to amend or reject "bad bills;" and (C) the Governor would either sign or veto legislation. This organizational structure would prove especially conducive for the budgetary process.

The American Revolution

The State Bureaucracy

The state government currently lists forty departments.[16] The various departments of the state should be few – no more than eight -- and should be stripped of either legislative and/or judicial powers. It is commonplace for legislators to draft laws with vague references to their enforcement and execution. Under these circumstances, civil servants who work in these departments have evolved them into mini legislatures who also have the power to render judgement and impose fines and other punishments without true due process of law. Many state agencies can send citizens a "ticket," which essentially convicts them of a crime and leaving it up to them to either admit guilt or to sue the state to prove their innocence, an act fundamentally contrary to American legal tenets. One is *always* assumed innocent until proven guilty. If an agency or department believes that anyone has violated the law, his/her only recourse should be to send such information to the Justice Department and recommend prosecution.

Moreover, the bureaucracy must be better automated. There is a wide variety of technological advances that could replace many people who currently slow down daily life in California, which is not that bureaucrats are bad people or even bad at their jobs. The reality, however, is every sector of the economy must deal with automation, and government should be no exception. The idea taxpayers should be forced to pay more for work that could be done faster and cheaper is archaic at best and deplorable at worst.

---

16 https://www.ca.gov/agenciesall/ There is so much duplication it is ridiculous. Multiple agencies doing virtually the same thing.

Don De Angelo

The most contentious factor with public employees is the benefits and job protection afforded them. Again, every part of America's workforce faces the reality of operational cost. Few, if any, private organizations can afford pensions, let alone the gold-platted ones offered to public employees. There must be a way to make this truth fit into the compensation given to public workers.

To realize this truth the pension system must be replaced with a defined contribution system. There is no way that one could legally or morally take such a benefit away from those who are either currently in retirement or close to ending their working careers. However, gradually eliminating pensions needs to occur.

First, the current contribution liability must be fulfilled. Even if the funds needed must be financed by a bond measure, all state and local public employees must be given the comfort in knowing the existing funds are at par and those retired civil servants who are dependent on the retirement funds will not be left in the lurch. There can be no exception to this rule as it has been an on-going crime for the various governments to underfund these benefits continually and knowingly. The behavior contributes to union rhetoric of foul play and less-than-honorable legislative intentions. Under such perceptions, the logical strategy of those unions is to push for promises of ever higher benefits that everyone already knows are unaffordable. Since most of the current deciders will inevitably be gone when the fiscal catastrophe hits, there is little risk to either side.

Second, the transition must be as smooth as possible to create buy-in and reduce hard feelings of long-term workers. Hypothetically, one would start by allowing those public employees 50 years of age and older to remain in the current system. There

The American Revolution

may need to be a "contribution" made by these employees to give added financial protection to the fund's viability, but the benefit should remain the same (and again, be fully funded per year and not have "IOUs"). Those workers from ages 35-49 would be given half the current benefit, and they would be allowed to contribute to a defined contribution plan. These individuals would be making a heavier contribution and should be considered for higher pay to compensate. Those government workers under the age of 35 should be moved to a fully defined contribution plan. There could be a variation of this process, including proposals to have the gradation done by decade or even yearly percentage shifts. Whatever process can pass the legislature is what should move forward as quickly as possible. All employees should be put onto Social Security (a system that also needs to be phased out), and 401(k)-type retirement plans, giving each person added savings for retirement and acting as a "safety net."

The following descriptions of departments are products of *streams of consciousness* thinking and not a definitive prescription of what must be done to heal the structural problems of any state, let alone one as large as California.

Department of the State: The primary purpose of such a body should be to organize and to manage the hiring and firing of public employees – the human resources department of the government. It should also keep all official government records and share of that information with the public.

The Department of the State should certify all election results and regulate ballot initiatives and referendums. The current system, which gives the California Attorney General the power to determine the wording of propositions, is either a misguided attempt at trying to control direct democracy or legalized voter manipulation.[17]

Finally, the department should promote the state, advertising state attractions organizing business conventions. Ideally, chambers of commerce, which do an excellent job, should do most of the work. The state should participate to ensure factual promotion of the state and to act as a coordinator among the counties and cities.

Department of Justice: The state's attorney general should no longer be elected separately. Instead, the governor should appoint this position with confirmation by the state senate. The sole responsibility of the AG should be to manage the prosecution of state law, with Civil Rights, Family Law, Property Protection, Business Regulation, Criminal Acts, and Environmental Law divisions. No individual department of the state should be permitted to issue punishments to any entity in the state. Perceived violations of law should be forwarded to the California Department of Justice, where the AG would determine if prosecution should move forward. No one should be presumed guilty without due process of law.

The state of California should be the first to decriminalize all drugs, focusing on recovery not incarceration. The California Department of Justice (CDOJ) should still cooperate with federal agencies (this being the case only so long as the federal government insists on continuing its war on drugs) around issues of drug trafficking. Most of the drug policies of the state should be left to county health commissions.

---

17   https://www.sfchronicle.com/hdn/hrlm/p/callback.html The practice has become blatant and near criminal!

The American Revolution

California should eliminate the death penalty, which has been an issue for decades with various governors toying with whether to commute death sentences or to push for more executions. The policy is expensive to sustain and is the absolute worst possible exercise of government power. No government should have the power over life and death, the ultimate form of tyranny.

Speeding on California freeways has become a varsity sport! When drivers exceed 75 miles per hour, yet multiple people whiz by, the law is not being respected. Meanwhile, it becomes demeaning to expect highway patrol personnel to pull over people and fight with them over behavior and/or punishment(s). The far more dangerous behavior on our freeways is those who drive erratically, weaving in and out of lanes of traffic at high speeds. It seems better to approach this with two priorities. First, issue citations to those who are clearly driving in dangerous fashion. Speeding can be part of that assessment. Secondly, should a driver cause an accident of any kind and it is determined that their speed was above what is considered "safe" there should be an additional penalty assessed. In other words, authorities need to treat drivers like adults and allow them to exercise responsible driving without too much interference, punishing those who are clearly endangering the public, especially those driving under the influence of any drug.

The state should end laws on vices. We are spending a lot of money trying to stop prostitution and other "sex" crimes. If there is an exchange of money for a sexual act between two consenting adults, it seems as though no crime has been committed. The focus of law enforcement should be to end trafficking in children for the sex industry and trafficking in anyone for slave-like activity. This element of society should be pursued with overwhelming force of law. It should also be illegal to be a "pimp." What a woman (or man) does with their body is up to them. If the transaction is between consenting adults the government should stay out. This is another reason why such social issues are best handled in private associations, especially religious ones. If you are to change the moral conduct of rational adults, it is only successfully accomplished in such arenas.

Germany is a good example of what to do and not do in this regard. Sex workers are legal in the country resulting in a steady increase in various forms of "sex resorts." The government was able to reduce prosecutions and there are various data to show that the general population is unharmed. However, the German government did not properly contemplate the influx of women trafficked into the country for the sex industry.[18] Without the proper focus on what could go wrong and how a more liberal system would be exploited, the government has found itself behind the eight ball. If any state is to relax its laws on sex work there must be a vigorous preparation to guard against sex trafficking, especially of children.

Department of Health: This department should become a center of innovation and education. California is such a large state that various regions will require different types of medical needs and ways of distributing healthcare. The state should monitor such activity and provide easy access to research and educational materials for the counties and private healthcare providers.

The department should wield oversight to ensure that the counties are providing the health services demanded by their

18 https://www.dw.com/en/germany-slow-to-tackle-human-trafficking-rights-evaluators-find/a-49279005

citizens and that the distribution of benefits is equitable and fair. It can be very easy for 58 separate counties to recede from an obligation if the perception is that no one is watching.

The only possible direct role for the state in healthcare might come in providing catastrophic health insurance along with short and long-term disability insurance. It is perhaps better to have this handled at the county level, which will be discussed later.

Department of Education: First, it would be worth investigating whether California schools' benefit from federal funds versus what it costs us to administer services? The Public Policy Institute reports that in 2018 the federal government provided a mere nine percent of total costs of K-12 education.[19] At what point does it become cheaper to refuse federal help and get rid of all the red tape requirements, instead of taking so little money with such large strings attached?

Nothing exemplifies a valued public good more than education. When a young United States was contemplating what to do with the new territory ceded to it by Great Britain, they made certain to include schools. For every township created in the Northwest Ordinance (1785) one 640-acre plot was set aside for a public school. It provided enough land upon which to build a school, and additional property to be sold to finance its construction and staffing of teachers. This was unheard of in the eighteenth century.

The role of the federal government was significantly limited. The law bestowed the land to the local government. Once

---

19   https://www.ppic.org/publication/financing-californias-public-schools/
Are we really in need of these funds, especially if we have to maintain large bureaucracies to administer them? And why does the Lottery only provide one percent?

Don De Angelo

schools were up and running the Congress kept out. The Morrill Act (1862) was a similar law done for state "land" colleges (think original Big Ten colleges). The first major investment by the federal government was in the Eisenhower administration. It was done in response to perceived dearth of engineers needed to close the "missile gap" with the Soviet Union after the launch of *Sputnik* in 1957. Infusions of federal money were made to build newer schools and construction of laboratories. The Advanced Placement program was begun to offer college-level curriculum to better prepare students for the rigors of university math, science, and English.

While federal spending on K-12 education has risen exponentially since the 1970s, when President Jimmy Carter created the Department of Education, there has been no marked increase in the performance of American students.[20] The greater the distance between those who impact curriculum and those who complete it; the greater the failure to demonstrate knowledge. Any private school with such outcomes would have to shut its doors.

Solutions seem distant because those who currently make the decisions could be literally hundreds of miles away. This is why education must be sent back exclusively to the local level (county or municipal). Publicly funded colleges and universities should be addressed by the state because they are funded by statewide taxes. In both instances, the tuition money should follow the student. Parents should have free reign in choosing where their child goes to school. Only an open voucher system, which allows

---

20   https://www.cato.org/cato-handbook-policymakers/cato-handbook-poli cy-makers-8th-edition-2017/47-k-12-education#a-brief-history-of-federal-in volvement

The American Revolution

all schools public and private to compete, will force the reforms necessary. There is no incentive in the current public K-12 school system to change.

What hopefully ends is any funding for Marxist ideological nonsense such as *critical race theory (CRT)*, *diversity equity and inclusion (DEI)* programs, *or environmental social and governance (ESG)* standards. None of these adds one point to any young person's grade point average. Any time spent on these indoctrination efforts is a disaster. The money currently spent in them would go a long way to fund art and music programs, which add significantly more value to a child's education. Schools are there to teach students how to think and not what to think. Critical Race Theory is just Marxist "critical theory" with race added in to give it a purpose. It is all poison.

It would be a fantastic project to find a way to incorporate the classical educational standards into our most current research on how students learn best. There needs to be a restructuring of education in general with a focus on community standards of ethics and developing an adult who can think for themselves and pursue whichever future path they hope will bring them happiness. There are some ideas that could help make these goals achievable.

Pre-K students should only be in a forced education structure if they are already demonstrating learning deficiencies. Delayed speech and inability to identify letters or numbers could be an issue of concern. Children from immigrant or lower income families often struggle in these areas and it would be helpful to intervene. There is not much to suggest that mandatory Pre-K is needed, and an ideal situation would be a natural gathering of toddlers who are permitted to interact and learn together with their parents and siblings. In other words, allow them to be toddlers. Kindergarten is a great place to start formal learning and should still be a playful environment.

Grades 1-5 need to be focused on skills. Remove electronic devises as much as possible and go back to the basics. There is nothing wrong with enhanced learning and creative arts, such as art and music, are critical to those basic skills. It would be great to start requiring lessons in logic along with math and scientific method. These are done in current schools, but the science is getting too political and there seems to be no logic at all.

Middle schoolers should be placed into a very rigorous program of specific courses and testing to gauge skill levels and aptitude for scholastic versus vocational learning. It would be great to either teach Hebrew, Greek, and Latin or at least classes on etymology. Literature should be the classics and that should include the Bible. In connection to Part I, young people should learn from where their rights come. There is no need for religious proselytizing. The focus should be on applying the skills they know into practical learning scenarios.

High school needs to radically change. The first two years should continue the rigors of middle school with attention spent on aptitudes. In the second (Sophomore) year, all students should have to pass a *general education degree* (GED) exam. They should also take the PSAT and the Armed Forces Vocational Aptitude Battery (AFVAB). These should help parents, students, and counselors determine a path forward. The second year should be a combination of general education classes and specialized work in their strength areas. Separated focus on either traditional high school, talent-vocation programs, and college preparation would allow a stronger effort to be applied to whichever path students choose.

The American Revolution

For example, high school students with an aptitude and desire for college should be taking all their universal course requirements BEFORE leaving for college. This can be done with regular teaching staff who have MA degrees in their subject areas and/or done through early college programs at local community colleges. The BA program would then only require three years of study, which would be an incredible savings for most families. The community colleges would also provide remediation for those students who may not exhibit the drive or ability for college until they are older.

The idea is that we need to start taking all paths of learning and life pathways seriously. When we make an unrealistic goal, such as all students will be college ready when they turn 18; we are creating barrier to learning because very few children will ever meet that standard. The eventual attitude will be to turn off to any schooling at all. Why be engaged if the outcome is already baked in – failure. Regular high schooler should be taking general education courses and picking up a part-time job. It could be a graded class where they are encouraged to do their best and demonstrate hirable behavior while earning some money.

Even the school schedule seems dated. Start by making Mondays for school administrative work and teacher meetings. A great idea is to open the schools to local religious communities to come on campus and teach ethics and morality classes for students who belong to their respective faiths. Make it easier for children to be exposed to learning how to be a good person. Tuesday through Friday should be the regular school week. This way, all holidays can be observed on Mondays and thus never lose classroom time.

Don De Angelo

Another suggestion would be an adjustment to the semester system. There should be a ten-week term, followed by a break and then a four-week *intersession*. This would be used for either enhancement courses or remediation for those students who failed to meet standards in the previous term. Repeat this for the spring. This way those students who are struggling can keep up with their peers. This would be especially useful in math, science, and language classes.

Regardless of how extensive reforms need to be, local communities should be the laboratories. Keep the federal government, and its money, out of it. States should focus on the state colleges and universities and make excellence the only goal.]

(CA case study) Under a *federalist* structure, the state government assumes full administration of the University of California (UC) and the California State University (CSU) systems. The Regency has not lived up to expectations. There are far too many current/pending examples of fraud in these budgets that could be funneled into lower tuition for in-state students. When you investigate the total compensation for administrators, who do zero teaching, you wonder who decided this was an "educated" decision?[21] Meanwhile, students are constantly complaining that so many of their professors are adjunct (part-time) and hard to reach outside of class. Is this the socialist utopia promised by so many elites in the ivory tower?

The department should differentiate between the two systems. The focus of CSU institutions should be to help lower income,

---

21 https://www.bizjournals.com/sanfrancisco/news/2017/10/26/all-the-university-of-california-500000-earners.html#g/422870/1 The saddest part is that UC and CSU are not that bad comparatively speaking. How sad is that?

The American Revolution

first generation, and underrepresented groups earn a bachelor's degree. The cost should be minimal, and admissions restricted to those students who earned a "C" average in their weighted GPA and a slightly competitive score on standardized exams. It would be most advisable for the state Department of Education to devise its own admissions exam if it does not feel confident in the existing ACT and SAT programs.[22] The CSU should have limited MA programs and no PhD programs.

The UC system should be reserved for California's most promising academic students. These scholars should have achieved at least a 3.75 GPA or higher, with exceptional talents in other areas (sports, music, art, engineering, etc.). No qualified California student should have to borrow money to attend a UC school. The state should make this system extremely competitive and charge out-of-state students very high tuition.[23] In order to control costs for the UC, there should be a privatization of all residential facilities. The sale of the dorms and dining halls would generate billions of dollars that could be placed in an endowment fund for off-setting tuition.

UC schools would be where most master's degrees and all PhD programs would reside. It would also house the medical, law, and other professional schools. There are way too many programs in the existing system and the multiplicity of state-sponsored programs are making each degree worth less in the marketplace and costing the state a great deal in duplicating administration. It would be great for ONE bureaucracy, fully automated, that

---

22 The controversy over standardized testing has become yet another strawman to avoid the larger question of failed education at the K-12 level.

23 Much of current student debt is a consequence of paying for living expenses not tuition.

Don De Angelo

could handle the admissions of both systems. Students could submit one application and the department would determine which school fits best for that student.

Having the California Department of Education create standards for admission to these schools will allow the counties to decide how best to educate their children to maximize their admission into either the UC or CSU. The counties' ability to help their students would be enhanced by giving counties control over the community colleges and vocational schools. More on this in the "Counties" chapter.

Department of Welfare: The California Department of Welfare should exist solely for oversight of county programs. The state should audit county files to ensure fraud is not occurring at any level. The department should also operate an appeals office where citizens may seek to overrule a county's denial of benefits.

Department of Commerce: There is way too many offices, departments, commissions, and whatever else associations in the state for the purpose of regulating business. This bureaucratic abyss has created an environment that stifles innovation and literally chases companies out of the state as soon as they begin to be profitable.[24] This is a department that needs major renewal. The best thing is to get rid of all other agencies that deal with commerce and have just ONE department.

There could easily be separate divisions based on economic sectors: agriculture; Manufacturing; mining; energy; travel and tourism; entertainment; high tech; transportation. Have all

---

24   https://www.pacificresearch.org/californias-business-climate-continues-to-receive-poor-scores/ This list of references could go on forever. California is constantly at the bottom of the pile.

worker's rights protected in this department as well. The best recommendation is to have the state OSHA and Arbitration services in this department. The standard should be simple – "Do No Harm." Businesses should operate with the best intentions for themselves, their workers, their customers, and their communities. Should their actions cause harm in any way, the courts should be permitted to award damages to individuals, communities, and/or the state. If such settlements bankrupt a company, then so be it.

The mission of the Department of Commerce is to promote California as a safe yet lucrative place to do business. The burden of running any company in the state should be reasonable and predictable. Less red tape, fewer regulations, and more assistance for gathering information will make California "gold again."

Department of Transportation: First order of business: kill the bullet train -- an embarrassing boondoggle. There needs to be a realization that the project has more to do with the Democratic party's deep-rooted connection to the construction unions than to any lofty goals of carbon sequestration or economic stimulus. There are way too many other things to be done in this state to be bothered by such a loser. If there is ever a truly lucrative way to have such transportation in the state, a private enterprise will step up to the plate. The fact that virtually zero private investors are coming forward should be the sign that this project is "dead-on-arrival."

The time has come to have just one agency deal with the roads, bridges, and freeways. The state should maintain all city streets, county roads, and state highways. Let one, state-wide automobile registration and gas tax pay this bill. Keep the paving privatized and have every roadway on a regular schedule. There are some very innovative surfaces being offered and already existing equipment to make this process faster and cost-effective. Stop diverting gas tax money to stupid projects and there should be enough to do the trick. Once there is a clear connection between a tax and a service, opposition to such taxes will be reduced. Most consumers understand a "user fee" is different than paying a tax that is never really earmarked.

If anything, good has come out of the COVID-19 pandemic it is the realization that nearly 50 percent of business can be done online with little to no ill effect on business. Should this practice be encouraged, California could see traffic and carbon emissions reduced by nearly half. This far exceeds any projections from mass transit investments. It would be far more cost effective to improve the internet connections and make them universal in the. Spend the money on the future economy and stop trying to recreate the transportation network of the 1940s. It would make a major contribution to the fight against climate change.

Shipping ports and airports should be self-funding enterprises. The state should be collecting fees from transportation companies and traveler-funded tax receipts to cover the costs of maintaining these facilities. If they are not, then the rates/fees should be increased to make sure that they do.

Department of Environment: The department should be divided into areas of concern: (A) Agricultural; (B) Industrial; (C) Natural; (D) Domestic; (E) Energy. The department should be regulating the uses of various chemicals and other artificial materials, which pose a threat to the national environment and the safety of the people.

Agricultural issues should be focused on the pesticides and fertilizers used in the production of food. These standards should

The American Revolution

be monitored, and violations reported to the Department of Justice for prosecution. Violators should be given written warnings about their infractions prior to filing with the Department of Justice.

Industrial pollutants create a constant worry, necessitating a list of products and materials forbidden for any use in the state. This department should monitor products that can be used under safe conditions. Maintaining an easy-to-use website on these substances will be a major part of this work. The mission should be to provide up-to-date information and educational materials to avoid potential problems in the first place. The assumption should not be that everyone is out to destroy the environment and therefore subject to constant surveillance and punitive oversight.

The department also should be responsible for the natural interior of the state. All current coastal commission responsibilities should be moved to this department and the preservation of natural spaces and state parks, reserves, forests, and beaches should be under its control. The best practice would be to unload any lands currently under state ownership that are associated with an existing Indian tribe, thus giving back to those from whom they were stolen. Indian tribes can manage these lands just as well as the government, perhaps much better. As long as parks and beaches remain open to the public, this arrangement allows Indians to diversify their income sources and maintain their heritage.

Energy is a sticky issue. Modern societies should aspire to maximize power with virtual zero fossil fuels. This goal is said not as an anti-fossil fuel initiative, but rather a better environmental perspective. Even if one does not buy into the climate change hysteria, clean air and less waste of limited resources makes sense.

Don De Angelo

The state should promote self-sufficiency at every level. If a private residence or business can use solar panels and/or wind turbines to take themselves off the grid, they should be encouraged to do so. Taking demand off the power grid is a good move, as it benefits the wealthier citizens but also conserves the main power sources for the rest of the community.

Counties also should invest in garbage incineration. The idea that we allow landfills to grow and/or try to sell our plastic waste to Asia is a travesty. Clean ways to burn our garbage and generate electricity exists. Carbon sequestration also allows for virtually no emissions.[25] Toxic materials also could be destroyed in this manner although requiring expensive facilities to achieve zero risk.

Human waste also can be processed to generate methane gas, which generates electricity. The humus residue can be used for fertilizers and the treated water drained through natural ponds, a strategy already operational in Arcata, California.[26] Virtually all brown water could be harnessed to generate non-fossil fuel power and to create nature supporting areas that the public can enjoy.

The time has come for green activists to wake up and realize a very important truth. Solar and wind power will *never* provide 100% of the energy needs of users. The amount of energy we are

---

25   https://www.nationalgeographic.com/environment/2019/03/should-we-burn-plastic-waste/ Consider that we could use landfills solely for toxic materials and counties could sell energy to the grid.

26   https://www.cityofarcata.org/856/Wastewater-Treatment-Facilities-Improvem This facility created additional wetlands that improved aviary migration and new natural spaces for the public to enjoy.

The American Revolution

currently generated is so small and has done so much damage to natural habitats that this dream needs to die.

Solar and wind farms are killing entire species of animals while barely cutting carbon emissions. While it is never easy to admit an error, this was a big one. In a TED Talk in Berlin, Germany, environmentalist Michael Schellenberger gave credible reasons to quit the solar/wind mantra.[27] We can get to the same goal, but we need to embrace nuclear energy to make it happen. Many rational people are wary of nuclear energy, it is easy to understand the hesitation. Thorium nuclear power seems to be the cutting edge of this technology.[28] It is always the hope that nuclear fusion will be available at some point but for now this is the best way.

Current technology on Thorium nuclear power would enable California to be 100% green power within 20 years. The only roadblock is our own regulations against such plants. If the state gets out of the way, energy companies are ready to go. Imagine, with car traffic down 40%-50% and more using hybrid or total electric power; we could see a virtually fossil-fuel free state in one lifetime!

The state of California is too big and too diverse to imagine any one government doing a good job of maintaining universal standards and efficient economies. By limiting the state to certain logical powers and allowing for specialization, the system can be more open to innovation and creativity. It will also

---

27 https://www.youtube.com/watch?v=ciStnd9Y2ak Shellenberger has several great talks on this and other climate issues.

28 https://www.youtube.com/watch?v=8nUjvpxzFbk

nurture more democracy as local communities make choices on how to run their SHEWs.

By helping people realize that more of what concerns them is being done through institutions closer to where they live, we encourage more participation in the decision-making process, and ease anxiety over potential tyranny and raise confidence in government. The state has become the jack-of-all-trades-and-the-master-of-none. This needs to change if we are to save the Golden State.

County Governments as the Center of Activity

In a federalist system of government, the decision-making power is divided to allow for more specialization and to accommodate more democracy. As always, it must be emphasized that the SHEW is best handled in free associations of citizens. Libertarians appreciate such organizations as the most free and efficient agents for SHEWs. California's size and the diversity of its population makes such a division of labor logical. In such a system the governing body closest to the people is better placed to address their needs, making it necessary to empower counties. Moreover, surrendering traditional city powers to a county will ensure a fairer distribution of revenue to the various implemented programs.

Public Education: The Commissioner of Education should be involved in all learning from pre-K through job training, vocational school, and/or community college. Beneath this office should be a superintendent for each of the major levels of education: Pre-K through fifth grade; sixth through ninth; high school; vocational/job training; and community college.

The American Revolution

Allowing education to be run at the county level would ensure that revenues collected for education were distributed throughout the county, per student rather than per school district, which would consolidate bureaucracies to just one for each county. San Diego County, for example, there would oversee just one community college district rather than five. With current technology, most administrative functions can exist online. Each campus could have a resource center where students can go for face-to-face questions or concerns; but most students would not have to bother.

Debate will arise about whether local communities would feel excluded from their traditional roles as overseers of local schools. It makes sense to allow for community school boards to operate to advise administrators on how to spend distributed funds and which programs to offer. The key is to have the operational bureaucracy streamlined and administered at the county level.

The next element of this public service would be to reform how schools operate. If the goal is to ensure all students have access to the best possible school, then an open voucher system is the only option, as too many poor and minority students are trapped in a low-performing schools. Several private schools, especially parochial, have had to shut down inner-city schools because they cannot compete with publicly financed ("free") competition. The Catholic schools boasted amazing track records with improving the educational skills of traditionally underrepresented communities. An open voucher system would allow for these schools to reopen and to provide these students with the programs that have proven to work.

This policy would require a per-student approach to funding county education. The county Commission of Education would determine how much would be spent for each student in the county and a "credit" would exist to allow parents/guardians to determine where these funds would be spent.

Without detracting from the main point, education should be based on each student's skills and motivation. External expectations by anyone not immediately involved in that child's welfare should not be immediately relevant. With that said, the schools are not places of miracle outcomes. A child who demonstrates either a lack of skill or desire to learn will not excel at even the best institutions.

A successful educational system recognizes teachers must respect learners where they are at and not where instructors would expect or want them to be. There is no point in an expectation that "all high school graduates must be college ready." No school controls the input of student ability or determination. Viewing all students as college material is an unrealistic goal that places for too much pressure on students, parents, teachers, and administrators with little evidence that society is getting the desired outcome. Allow students to communicate where they are either academically or personally to determine educational pathways.

For example, consider a student who has a good academic ability, but poor motivation. The school could try pushing the student to do more and even punish him/her, but what is the usual result? The child perceives education as a negative force in his/her life and may even reject learning to rebel. Allowing the student to do what he/she is willing to do and able to perform well will come with a consequence – in this case, a limited number of post-secondary options. But, if the student completes the secondary education process, he/she can always return to post-graduate learning – vocational and/or community college

The American Revolution

– whenever he/she decides it is their best interest. At this point the student takes the learning process serious because he/she sees the benefit to his/her own aspirations.

This scenario unburdens teachers who were never meant to be saints but are continuously called upon to perform miracles just because someone asks for them. The stress on a committed educator to make every child the same is unrealistic and pushes many good teachers to leave the profession. Meanwhile, students, who have been told they can be as good at academics as anyone else and that college is an entitlement, subconsciously know they are not quite up to snuff, yet they attend college unprepared and destined for failure.

A modified-tract system is best suited to solve this problem. By tracking students throughout their school years and placing them in "tracts" that best suit their abilities and preferences, students will find niches and take whatever time they need to get educated. So long as the tracts are open to transferring in and out of them, then the process will be fair and more efficient.

Public Safety: This department should provide fire and police protection for the entire county as well as emergency services, such as ambulance and disaster response. By creating one administrative bureau for the county, the savings from smaller offices could result in higher pay for safety officers.

County sheriffs traditionally have run jails, prisons, and served as bailiffs in courtrooms. In this model, the sheriff's office would serve as the administrative arm for all law enforcement and safety personnel. Each community would retain their local police forces and fire departments, but the administration function would fall under one sheriff. A police chief would direct local forces and report to the county sheriff. Again, this set-up eliminates a lot of administrative duplication, redirecting recouped funds to attract more talented officers.

Public Welfare: There is a great deal of support for the idea of helping the poor, but seldom does that transfer into universal support for any one program. This area screams for creativity and compassion.

Currently, many interesting ideas are currently circulating that might be worth implementing. One plan allows citizens to contribute up to 2% of their salaries to a social welfare organization of their choice in their respective counties. This deduction would be prior to assessing other taxes. Many local social welfare groups would thrive if they could secure automatic contributions every payday. The consistent flow of capital would allow these groups to focus more on their stated missions rather than fundraising.

Universal basic income (UBI) is another idea coming from more socialist circles. If implemented, UBI needs to be done with clear parameters. The county would determine what annual salary is necessary for an individual to live comfortably. The county would pay financial support by taking an individual's income and subtracting it from the needed minimum.

UBI is not the best option for anyone who believes in libertarian forms of government, nor for anyone supporting Austrian economic theory. However, certain restrictions may be added to give the idea more clout. First, make sure only citizens of the United States would be eligible. Next, all recipients must be working at least 40 hours a week. We also do not want to create the impression that a UBI is a substitute for the hard work that should be associated with a basic income. Insisting recipients work full-time ensures that welfare is never seen as a "chosen" profession and keeps workers up to date on employment skills and trends.

The American Revolution

The third idea to better serve the poor is to be limited that total number of years an individuals can receive benefits. UBI should incentivize individuals to pursue additional training and/or use the financial safety net to transition into a new field of work without too much financial disruption. The final key factor is that this idea should replace all the other welfare programs: Food stamps, heat and renter's assistance and any cash transfers. There should be no minimum wage with such a system so that employers are encouraged to hire individuals that are normally excluded from the workforce because they need training or lack work experience.

There is some evidence that by using just one direct payment system would remove the need for the massive bureaucratic infrastructure that plagues local government. Eliminating staff means saving on salaries, benefits, and retirement obligations, which could mean a net gain for the taxpayers.

Public Sanitation: This agency also requires consolidation to save money on administrative overhead. Most garbage collection and disposal are done with private contractors and could be orchestrated at one level. The county government should create one functioning plan for such services rather than myriad local programs.

Sweden uses its garbage disposal to generate heating and electric power for its communities. Incinerating garbage can save landfills and power several homes. Iceland has devised ways to send carbon emissions from energy plants into the ground to sequester the greenhouse gases for added environmental value.

Separate collections should exist for compostable garbage so that more organic waste could be set aside and used for gardening on county properties. Recycling centers should remain a major part of the sanitation system but be restricted to those materials that are commercially valuable to the market. Often, using energy to recycle an unwanted product is more wasteful than incineration.

Brown water disposal also deserves a better approach. Arcata, California boasts an amazing system where sewage sludge is digested to produce methane gas used to generate electricity. The organic humus created can be used as a fertilizer and the water runoff can be filtered through a series of connecting ponds, creating new wetlands for migrating birds, ultimately leading to clean water draining into our rivers, lakes, and oceans.

Public Transportation: Since the streets of the entire state would fall under state authority, the country can focus its attention on infrastructure for busses and trains. Although train services are detrimentally expensive to build and inefficient to operate, some existing systems must remain to avoid too much disruption to the lives of people who have come to depend on them.

If counties desire to eliminate traffic congestion and carbon emissions, they should encourage employers to have as much work as possible done from worker's homes. During 2020's pandemic crisis, more than 40% of work was being done remotely and no one seemed to be saying it was unproductive.[29] Most existing mass transit systems have a goal of reducing commuter traffic of a much smaller number. With one simple program in place, a county could see massive reductions in carbon emissions and a much safer and friendlier traffic situation – all with minimal government spending.

---

29   https://www.mckinsey.com/featured-insights/future-of-work/whats-next-for-remote-work-an-analysis-of-2000-tasks-800-jobs-and-nine-countries#

The American Revolution

Public Health: The scope of public health should be limited to general services necessary to for a community to be well. Imposing a one-size-fits-all remedy is proving to be more costly and not as effective as imagined.

To improve the delivery of quality health care, the county should register local health care options. If the state provides basic short and long-term disability and catastrophic healthcare, then most carriers would be able to offer various family health club programs for consumers. An open market set up for medical services would encourage cost-based shopping, which would eventually lower the costs of most routine procedures. The current system does not incentivize people to price shop, and guaranteed payments (either from insurance companies or governments) mean providers simply perform as many procedures as possible to maximize profits.

The pandemic crisis certainly has raised the bar for what is expected of our public health services. Having proper testing kits and processes in place would have saved many lives and prevented a great deal of panic. If there is any genuine role for a government-run healthcare system, it is when society is confronted with such a crisis. There were also clear missed opportunities for health services to coordinate with public safety personnel, which should not be allowed to happen again. Preferably the government should concentrate on this first and let the rest of medical care fall into the real free market.

Public Parks and Recreation: The fun part of public service rests in providing the open spaces and community facilities for people to enjoy themselves. As such, this department should be county wide to save on administrative costs. At the risk of sounding like a broken record, there are too many ways to eliminate duplication among cities by combining the oversite into one office.

Don De Angelo

In a realistic plan of good government, local placement of social services seems the better route. Most government should be located as close to the taxpayers as possible. In a democratic republic, physical proximity to the center of power where decisions are made is ideal and should be encouraged. When you consider the distance of Washington, DC from California it is amazing that so many people here continue to support, and even demand, more national government programs.

Many might wish for no government at all, while others fear that without government someone might be abused or neglected. The balance seems to be to minimize the size of the bureaucracy, which tends to absorb most of the long-term costs. It is also important to have a government that is dedicated to review its own work and be willing to eliminate programs that are not always working and be open to free market options. Sunset clauses, which predetermine the expiration of a law, would be an excellent addition to all legislation.

The choice of placing most government at the county level is based on California's size and the future problem of public employee pension liabilities. If there were large governments at the state, county, and municipal level – the size of oppressive government grows ever larger. Fifty-eight regimes handling most social services seems a decent balance and could result in massive savings for taxpayers.

Role for City Government

The purpose of this exercise has been to envision a different path for government in California because if its unique size and

The American Revolution

diversity. In an ideal world it might be possible to have all sorts of governing bodies for various levels of public life (state, regional, county, and local). The cost of such a complex reality has caused the state to be mired in an odd mix of cost prohibitive programs and bureaucratic incompetence. To this discussion, the reduction of political entities to just two entities – state and county – is meant to address both problems without sacrificing utility.

If there still needs to be a city government, it would be for the purpose of promoting the urban culture for both local populations and tourists. In a very real sense, the best vehicle for such promotion should be done by those parties who are most to benefit from such activities. Hotels, restaurants, and entertainment enterprises should pool their own resources to promote participation. This frees up funds that are usually provided by local and state money. Every city and state in America have a chamber of commerce. Since the promotions most benefit its members why not insist, they bear the price?

The remaining interest of a city government would most likely be advocation of local interests before the county. As stated above, the county legislature should have an upper house composed entirely of persons elected as mayors. Their role would be to review proposed ordinances and either recommend their approval, suggest alterations to improve a bill, or completely refuse to move it forward. This would be a mayor's primary role.

The secondary role of a city mayor would be a ceremonial one. The mayor would be available for promotion of local activities and cultural events. It would be a good thing to have the mayor on a tourism board or development committee, perhaps a voting member of a chamber of commerce. The ideal is to have a mayor who is responsive to local advocacy and willingness to take voter's concerns to the Council of Mayors. The larger the city the more councilors will be in the county legislature. Mayors could then form a caucus to assist promotion of any ordinances favorable to local interests.

It may not be a possible form of government. It is crucial to view this as a proposal for discussion rather than a manifesto for action. The commitment is to find the best way to streamline the state's governing system and save taxpayers money. Fewer governing bodies should mean fewer restrictions on personal lives and economic development. Local governments have also been the center of a great deal of historical corruption, which creates a weary voting population. Redesigning a system with limited powers and delegated authority could be a way to prevent repressive systems and promote diversity and creativity.

Review of Reforms and Revisions

We must remind ourselves that all governments repress people and societies to some degree. The coercive power of government easily can be abused and create situations that build public unrest and resentment. To avoid such calamities, it is good for any people to review their political systems to ensure that it is the people who remain sovereign and not government institutions.

Taxation: A nice formula for revenue in California is to first review what is being asked of government. In a more limited expectation, certain revenue streams would be earmarked for each level of state government. The base should be a statewide flat tax of 5% and then add percentages by county and local considerations. More rural areas may not need to be any higher than 5%

The American Revolution

and could eliminate the property tax, which is a major obstacle to home ownership for lower income residents. Use the existing state Franchise Board to collect the taxes, and it must be a flat tax with no deductions.

Politicians and the public must come to terms with the truth that public services are not FREE. If Californians desire state provided healthcare, free tuition for community college, and greater safety nets for the poor – the cost must be borne by everyone. Historically, the idea that California can continue to tax the rich to provide comfortable lives for the middle and lower classes is a Robin Hood fantasy that has never been realized. The vision promoted by Democrats and socialists of a European utopia fails to explain the high costs associated with them.

Most Europeans pay at least 50 percent of their incomes in various taxes. Yes, the rich pay even more, but imagine if all Californians were told they had to cough up more of their own money, some who have never paid any taxes before. The narrative since I moved to the state in 1992 increasingly has been one of "soak those rich people who don't deserve it," which makes for good rhetoric, but it has proven to fall continually short of cash and never seems to correct targeted social ills. IF Californians wish to have such nice lives without relying on their own resources and talents, then it is imperative to begin explaining the true cost of such an existence.

The state should strive for fewer sources of revenue earmarked for specific purposes. First, a ten percent business income tax should ONLY be at the state level, and it should cover the cost of maintaining the regulatory apparatus of the state. Gas taxes and registration fees should cover highway and street maintenance. As many government programs as possible should depend on user fees.

Don De Angelo

Is there a better formula? Possibly. Again, this proposal is not dogma. The key elements of any restructuring program should be simplicity and designated streams of revenue. The more taxpayers can see their dollars spent on specific programs (i.e., their gas taxes paying for great roads and bridges), the less they complain about the tax burden. Flat income taxes will be appreciated every April when there are zero forms to fill out and/or audits to fear. Lower taxes and fewer reporting requirements will lower hostility toward taxes and those who impose them.

Sovereign Wealth Fund: There are tons of resources in the state of California. It is not called the Golden State just because of one commodity. Mining in the state has uncovered multiple ores needed for American industry. Forests and fisheries also have a high demand in the U.S. economy. The oil and gas industry will always have a role in the world and California will continue to exploit them both, even when we can all appreciate the value of dramatically lessening our dependency on them.

Considering the state's abundance, California officials have been negligent in creating future security from such resources. Norway was for many decades a poor country. Beginning in the 1970s, the discovery of oil and natural gas deposits has reversed their fortunes. Deliberate planning by the Norwegians placed a portion of the country's royalties into a fund, which has been invested internationally on behalf of the entire population. This fund, now has more than $1 trillion in assets, which translates to over $195,000 per Norwegian![30]

---

30   The Norwegians know their frugality will pay off: https://www.nbim.no/en/. https://en.wikipedia.org/wiki/Government_Pension_Fund_of_Norway

The American Revolution

The state of California has so much that is desired by the world, and we have squandered it on shiny things that will one day lose value. We need to start thinking about the future. This is not to be mistaken for the current "rainy day fund." This mythical creature is the rhetorical construct of the Democratic party trying to convince Californians that they can be trusted with even more tax dollars. Such funds are useful for temporary revenue shortfalls and nothing more. Let's take our royalties from all our natural resources and invest these monies for a prosperous future.

Direct Democracy: Little wonder exists as to why so many Californians loathe elections. The onslaught of propositions and referenda put forward is daunting and convoluted, many of those passed challenged in courts and costing millions of dollars even before they go into effect. Add the real costs that seem to only become real *after* the voting, and a recipe for disaster emerges.

To believe all voters dedicate the time and/or desire to sit down and fully contemplate the motivations and designs behind all proposed changes to California's constitution and/or laws is a wonderful thought. To hope the only people drafting such ideas are average voters is equally amazing. However, neither of these is true, prompting us to find a way to include the public in legislative processes while retaining the dignity expected.

There is a strong rationale for not allowing plebiscites except for amendments to a state's constitution. Direct democracy can not only devolve into ugly discourse, but it often leads to bad government at an incredible expense, while excusing legislators from doing their jobs. When a law fails people can blame responsible lawmakers. When a bad referendum or initiative flops, politicians easily excuse it as "the will of the people."

Don De Angelo

If the presumption is the people's direct voice is imperative to effective governance, then it becomes even more important to perform the job properly. As a result, a quorum must be required to legally bind any direct vote. Three-quarters of registered voters must participate in an election for any such vote to count. Any amendments to the state's constitution also should require a two-thirds approval. The imposition of such requirements will deter those members of the legislature trying to circumvent their own colleagues, thus ensuring a true base of support for such changes and lowering attempts by "anti" voters from launching lawsuits after election day.

Death to Commissions: No greater waste of money in California exists than the commission system. State legislators in their respective committees could easily oversee issues needing addressed. By expanding the number of assemblymen and senators per previous recommendation of more than doubling the state assembly, half of any given year could be devoted to process overview.

Commissions have become a dumping ground for political cronies and future political office-seekers. The amount of money wasted in these bodies is enough to finance the California State University system. If policy is being poorly implemented in the state, then those officials elected to handle such matters should and can be held responsible.

Too many layers of government strangle the state's ability to innovate and to respond to rapid world changes. Streamline the process for some government functions and end government involvement all together in other areas. Commissions and commissioners debilitate the state's economy and efficiencies of scale.

The American Revolution

To What Purpose?

It is never enough to say, "change it." While many people reflect romantically about revolutions and rebellions and their dramatic effects on society, they too often forget how many such actions fail miserably.

California is a state borne of dramatic action and innovative development. While far from perfect, the state proclaimed itself from its inception free of slavery and called to a better purpose. This state has given the world wealth, life-saving medicines, and some of the most creative artistic enterprises in human history.

In the whirlwind of such activity, it many citizens to easily assume the good times will last forever falling back on the belief that so many people want to live here that we can tax them and regulate them for as much money as we deem necessary to replenish the coffers.

This position is the major failure of the neo-Marxist world view overtaking our academic institutions, political elites, and mainstream media. The idea that limitless money abounds is politically unsustainable and intellectually immature.

The wealthy who we are told we must resent have never been a singular group of people conspiring to repress the masses. Most people who are rich rank as the most innovative, hard-working people in society. The downward mobility of the rich also is an issue that few, if any of us "poor souls," bother to investigate.

The wealthy are also the foundation of our employment. My career as an educator has been entirely dependent on the charitable acts of the well off. Thousands of lower income children have been educated at my private school because of it. No doubt it changed the course of an entire family's history to have such an opportunity.

Don De Angelo

The zero-sum mentality that has overtaken Sacramento has the potential to tarnish the Golden State. The people of Greece were some of the wealthiest in all of Europe if not the world. Shipping tycoons were the romantic figures of the 1950s (remember Jackie Kennedy Onassis?) What happened? Marxist militarists took over the government and implemented the same tax strategy as our Democratic leaders in Sacramento. The more they regulated and taxed the rich and productive, the more of them that left. When revenue dried up they resorted to borrowing. Eventually the amount they owed in interest payments was more than they could raise in taxes.

Greece has the same climate. It is still considered one of Europe's playgrounds. Tourists from all over the world flocked to its shores every year. And it is broke! Pensions have been cut in half and services have been reduced in every way possible. The people there are broken and looking for a new beginning. The government seems to have finally realized that it cannot make a silk purse out of a pig's ear, but they waited so long that the transition is extremely painful for everyone, especially the poor.

California has all the resources it needs and all the innovative and creative people it could possibly want. To sit down now and contemplate possible reforms will mean a level of prosperity that we have yet to imagine. We could do this without demonizing the rich or denigrating the poor. Let's have these conversations now before we are forced to accept drastic restructuring imposed from outside our state.

Gold needs to be polished to keep its shine. The work requires a willingness to spend the time and exert the energy. We are young, vibrant, and smart – time to roll up the sleeves and solve some problems.

PART 3

The National Revival

Don De Angelo

America the Republic

One of the first things that bother me about the national dialogue is just how less informed many people are about the structure of the United States government. When individuals call for "every voice to be heard," or that the people are "entitled" to certain parts of the nation's largess, I wonder where these people went to school. The idea that the federal government would ever be the end all American life is just pure fiction.

The Framers seemed to inherently understand that any government with enough power to do everything for everyone was also powerful enough to arbitrarily take rights and privileges away. England provided American colonists with significant military defense and in many cases babied their subjects in the New World to ensure that they could continue to stay in business. England *did* for many colonists what today's interest groups beg the current federal government to do – ensure that there is a minimal level of success so that one can count on a certain level of comfort.

This worked well for a very long time. Many colonists lived longer, healthier lives than their counterparts in the Mother Country. Some, like Benjamin Franklin, became noted movers and shakers on both sides of the Atlantic. So, it was somewhat of a surprise to Britain that these "United Colonies" wanted to be "free and independent States."

What "separated us one from the other," was a new notion of freedom. Peter Ornuf writes that Jefferson idealized America as a "rising empire…sustained by affectionate union, a community

107

The American Revolution

of interests, and dedicated to the principle of self- government."[31] The English Constitution relied on imperial and monarchial principles, which assumed sovereignty bequeathed to the people from an anointed lord and an elected parliament made up of propertied males and members of the peerage. The arbitrariness of this power was the foundation of American disquiet and uneasiness. It is one thing to focus on the cultural differences that emerged over centuries of separate living experiences. It is quite another to propose that this difference of lifestyle was enough to spawn a violent revolt against the greatest military empire in human history.

No, we must assume these were logical people. The ideals of liberty motivate far more than mere arguments over whether one spells it theatre or theater. The Enlightenment notion that everyone is sovereign and that the people relinquish some of their sovereignty to a government in a "social contract" was the true revolutionary concept. This new government was to be centered on the notion that each person was a master of his/her own destiny. Based on this ideal, the people not only control the outcome of government, but they also take command of their own lives. The government will guard and protect one's liberties but not nurture and subsidize one's sense of self-worth.

This is where Americans today get confused. We focus on the notion that "All men are created equal," and contort this to mean that we are all *equal*. Egalitarianism is so distorted in our minds that we take it to mean that each American must get the same as other Americans. This would be *equity*, which is impossible

---

31   Ornuf, Peter, *Jefferson's Empire: The Language of American Nationhood*, University Press of Virginia, Charlottesville and London: 2000, p. 1, 7.

Don De Angelo

to attain and require tyrannical government to attempt. This is socialism not republicanism. I am to be treated "equally" under the law, but any notion that I would get the same legal defense as Bill Gates is silly. Bill Gates has more in part because he was willing to risk more. The beauty of egalitarianism is that it gives all of us an equal chance to be Mr. Gates. It is also true that the success of a truly egalitarian society depends in part on the generosity of those who have more than others. But the idea that we must all have the same is a cop out. It excuses us from hard work and entrepreneurial thinking.

The misinterpretation of these principles has led to the formation of newer institutions in American government, which have distorted and tainted republican democracy. While Madison agreed that factions are mostly based on the "unequal distribution of property," he believed that pure democracy, "can admit no cure for the mischiefs (sic) of factions," created by the discord.[32]

And yet, this has been the trend in American politics since the Progressive Era. We want everyone to be equal and so we have created institutions to "improve" democracy. The referendum, recall, and initiative are all great examples of attempts to create a greater sense of equality at the expense of republicanism. In the case of California, any analysis of the state must conclude that most of the state's problems come from the litany of laws passed by various degrees of direct democracy. These "acts" have imposed expenses upon the legislature, a bizarre type of entitlement, which complicates the budget process and prevents state government from making responsible fiscal choices.

---

32   Madison, James, *Federalist 10*

The American Revolution

Even the notion of term limits has a negative effect upon the notion of republicanism. At the very foundation of representative government is the idea that citizens are in control over who they choose to speak on their behalf. Term limits are meant to tell a constituency that the rest of the country has decided to limit their options in the interest of other Americans unhappy with the power of other representatives. It is a truly distorted sense of equality – "I feel left out of the political process and so it must be that these other district leaders are manipulating the system with their longevity. Therefore, if I take away longevity, I secure my equality." The reality is that such thinking deprives the people of their most basic political right – to choose whomever they wish to sit in the national assembly. The other affect is to create a legislature filled with individuals unfamiliar with the workings of government or more concerned with the next step in their own political career. They either wallow around in their ignorance of process or fall prey to lobbyists who are not limited to any "term" and stay around long enough to control outcomes.

The unintended consequences of movements based upon the notion of "leveling the playing field" is the expanding power of the *deep state*. Some who study the plight of the poor and underrepresented turn their frustrated energies on the government, looking for simple answers to complex questions about society. If it is a perceived lack of voice, we give them the vote (people under 21 for instance), even when they continue to have problems and fail to vote in huge numbers. We impose affirmative action to undo past injustice on generations long dead and then ignore inherent societal issues that are far more relevant to the progress of individuals in any group. Again, public employees get more influence and power along with lucrative careers, but little else really gets accomplished.

And the equalizing gets so complex that it begins to come into conflict with itself. In education, the progressive spirit has called for the nation's schools to do miracles every day with assets far from miraculous. The reason is that the same people who want ALL Americans to have the same high-quality education comes face-to-face with the even louder cry to equalize the financial and professional standing of teachers. We have created a monopoly in education and ask it to do the unselfish act of teaching everyone the same. These are two conflicting ideals. The teachers' unions are given the power to influence politicians through their fundraising and lobbying, which gives them power over the cost of learning, only to then limit what its customers can do to ensure they get what they paid for.

Not only does this perpetuate a system of mediocrity, but it also dumps an ever-increasing cost on an already overburdened government. The national agenda becomes ever longer, and the price tag continues to grow. Losing grip of the former creates greater pressure upon the latter. Well intentioned as it may be, demanding a government that is perpetually obsessed with making everyone feel good about themselves and their role in society makes for very bad government and a disgruntled people.

The answer is to return to the simplicity of the original Framers. These were men who understood full well the unfairness of life. Many toiled for decades only to see their fortunes sucked into the English treasury via taxes and a lopsided balance of trade. Some had come to the New World as indentured servants and would have loved a more consistent set of rules over their treatment. And yet they came to the idea of a federal government

The American Revolution

only when they felt that their very lives and fortunes depended on it. Even then the Constitution was written in a way that was supposed to significantly limit the powers of the national regime.

And then there are those who want to strip the document of any semblance of power. The Articles of Confederation was a construct with zero national sovereignty. This first framework of government reflected a natural fear of any centralized authority. All sovereignty rested with the states, which bestowed certain powers to the Continental Congress concerning a united defense and foreign policy. Many in the MAGA or Tea Party movements seem to be thinking of this document when calling for the shrinking of the federal government. This is a misplaced sentiment because the Framers were certainly conscious of the fact that the new Constitution created a separate, sovereign (national) government with its own powers, which were intended to be superior to the states.

The dilemma today is to find the truth behind everyone's position. Progressives are misguided in assuming additional powers for the federal government every time they feel there is some wrong to be righted or great idea that needs national support. This abuse of the *Necessary and Proper Clause* would offend the Framers who were very intentional in their preference for national authority, but always accommodated the idea of limited government and promoted the concept of "reserved powers" for the states to ensure that federal intrusion into the lives of every day Americans was minimal.

Modern anarchists become obsessed with zero government to the point where one wonders if there will be any program that can survive the fiscal axe. If government dwindles too far, too fast, there will be no authority left to give the American people

Don De Angelo

the confidence that national power has any legitimacy to protect the people's rights to life, liberty, and property. Too much *power of the people* will inevitably lead to what the Greeks called *chaos* and what Aristotle called *democracy*. The current government is far too large, but at some point, the cutters begin to remove muscle and bone, something Federalist like Hamilton feared would invite rebellion and civil war.

Simple ideals need to be agreed upon. First: the country was never meant to be governed directly by the people. Republicanism calls for people to elect a representative to vote on their behalf and, so long as the constitutionally prescribed process is followed, we the people consent to obey. If the sentiment of the public will, as enacted into law has somehow violated the constitution the federal courts can "review" such legislation.

Second, the federal government was given certain enumerated powers that from time to time may require additional authority. But the Constitution also made clear that powers not ascribed to the national regime are reserved for the states or the people (Amendment X). Ever since the Progressive Era this tenant has been stripped down to where it barely has any credible bearing on American government. Madison feared this concentration of power and, in a matter of ten years after writing as a Federalist, he switched his allegiance and became a Republican (Anti-Federalist). The only way to check federal corruption is to disperse power to states and municipalities to starve the national regime and keep political factions in constant competition for power.

It is not enough to lament the crisis of government inefficiency. All government is inefficient to some degree. It is seldom the goal of politicians to be agile but to be as fair as possible and as

The American Revolution

beneficial to as many citizens as one can. This is hardly a formula for cost effectiveness.

The real problem is us -- the voters. We have bought into the idea that government is the place of first and last resort. We have placed upon the government the unrealistic expectation that some nebulas force of authority will have the answers to all our difficulties. So, we continue to want the government to do for us while we simultaneously become frustrated at the wasted billions (and now trillions) of dollars. We then get ourselves in the odd position of refusing to approve tax increases while we insist that none of our pet-programs be cut. We create this dilemma by having wrong expectations because we have lost sight of what our government was constitutionally constructed to be.

The basics shall set us free. By remembering that the Constitution was written to create a republican government that would handle the most basic needs of the nation, we begin to lower our own expectation. When we begin to rely on ourselves and one another for our daily lives, we take the pressure off Washington by lowering the demand for more government. This permits the government to shrink and become more manageable, and less expensive. State and local governments can take on whatever responsibilities its constituent's desire. The Tenth Amendment assumes just that. This basic understanding needs to be embraced by Americans first before any real, long-term solutions can be implemented.

Balance of Powers

Once we accept that we live in a republic we can begin to examine what the Constitution has to say about power. The

Don De Angelo

idea of limited government was the truly revolutionary idea of our Founders. The tyranny of British authority convinced the Founders of two main concepts of American political culture: political power must be expressed on paper, and it must be limited as much as possible.

Thomas Jefferson was a major figure among the Founders and yet was not at the Constitutional Convention. He was the ambassador to France. When writing about the mere idea of creating a stronger central power he reflected that, "the only thing worse than one tyrant in London, will be 200 tyrants in Philadelphia." To many of the Framers[33], there was no greater threat to the country's, newly found liberty than to concentrate power in one government, farther removed from the people.

Most Americans probably take the idea of a "balance of power" in reference to international relations – a theory that explains how countries maintain relative world peace. But the American constitutional make-up deals with the same notion in many contexts. The first is the balance of power within the three branches of government. This derived from our suspicions that the British model of all power of government based essentially in one branch (Parliament) in one central location (London) was too corrupt. Our Founders embraced the Enlightenment idea of separating government power into legislative, executive, and judicial branches as the best protection against tyranny.

33　It is interesting to note the use of terms, such as "Founder" and "Framer". A Founder is any member of the Revolutionary period who supported the drive for independence. A Framer is a very specific person – one who attended the Constitutional Convention. Many people assume certain Founders were present at this event and that contributes to misunderstandings.

The American Revolution

The next division is that between the national and state governments. This "federalism" is the notion that each state of our Union is a separate, sovereign power, which has chosen to embrace the U.S. Constitution and all its benefits and limitations. The proof of support for this interpretation comes in the "full faith and credit" clause of Article IV. Section I demands that all the states, respect each other's authority. If the federal constitution enshrines state sovereignty within its pages, is it not recognition that the states would retain certain exclusive rights? This was important to the Framers as a way of using the new national government as an "umpire" among the states to end the chaos that had been created during what John Quincy Adams referred to as the *Critical* Period.[34]

The power of the federal government to control interstate relations is the main impetus for the Supremacy Clause, which gives final constitutional authority to the national regime. If it were the intention to secure *sole* supremacy of federal law, the states would have been replaced by one centralized government. This was clearly not done. Instead, the Framers decided to allocate specific *expressed* powers to the federal government and *reserve* the remaining powers to the states.

There remained a sticking point. The powers that only the federal government possess, are enumerated in Article I, Section VIII. At the end of this list is the *Necessary and Proper* Clause.

---

34 The notes of various Framers can be very instructive. Federalists, which included Madison at the time, saw the economic and political unrest a direct threat to the independence of the country. Madison even argued for a strong enough navy to be able to sail it into the harbors of intransigent states to force their compliance to the national will. John Q. Adams reflected this perception in his July 4th address.

Don De Angelo

The verbiage grants to Congress, "To make all Laws which shall be necessary and proper for carrying into Execution the foregoing Powers, and all other Powers vested by this Constitution in the Government of the United States, or in any Department or Officer thereof." Essentially, the Framers wanted to make sure that the federal government could perform its constitutional duties without having to perform prolonged legal battles with or interference by the states.

All the expansions of federal power we study have derived from a "loose" interpretation of this phrase, which is now commonly referred to as the *Elastic Clause*; because the government can merely "stretch" the meaning of the constitution to derive the authority desired. The Antifederalists were most alarmed by this small sentence at the bottom of a very long list.

Many Americans forget that drafting the Constitution was just the first hurdle. To ensure that the new government would have the legitimacy to govern on its own without state interference; the Framers insisted that each state allow its residents to elect conventions for the purpose of ratifying the new constitution. While many members of these conventions were also members of the state legislatures, the point was that the process was done outside of the state political system.

The *Federalist Papers* were a set of articles written in newspapers by those who wanted a stronger central government and therefore ratification of the Constitution. What few students are ever exposed to are the writings by the Antifederalists who feared the new system would lead to a tyrannical, concentrated power far removed from the people. Their arguments, called by default the *Antifederalist Papers*, are an interesting 18th century critique that is hauntingly like present day reality.

The American Revolution

In reviewing the Necessary and Proper Clause, Antifederalist "Brutus"[35] expresses fear that this and the Supremacy Clause meant, "The government, so far as it extends, is a complete one," meaning singular and supreme. The phrasing of these clauses is so vague that any Congress, "may so exercise this power as entirely to annihilate all the state governments and reduce this country to one single government."[36]

Brutus continues by projecting forward to an ever-growing American republic. Should the nation physically grow as the federal government's power increases, "it is impossible to have a representation, possessing the sentiments, and of integrity, to declare the minds of the people, without having it so numerous and unwieldly, as to be subject in great measure to the inconveniency of a democratic government." The support of the people in their government will diminish because, "The confidence which the people have in their rulers, in a free republic, arises from their knowing them, from their being responsible to them for their conduct, and from the power they have of displacing them when they misbehave."[37]

And a central government physically distant from most of its people and so small will not "be acquainted with the local condition and wants of the different districts, and if it could, it is impossible it should have sufficient time to attend to and

---

35 In the 19th Century, it was common place for writers of social and political commentary to use pseudonyms instead of their real names. This was done to both protect writers from severe punishment in places where free speech was restricted and to appear to be less self-promoting (your ideas were supposed to speak for themselves). Many of the Founding Fathers/Framers used names of famous Greek or Roman philosophers.

36 Brutus No. I, October 18, 1787.

37 Idem

Don De Angelo

provide for all the variety of cases of this nature, that would be continually arising."[38]

The result would be representatives who fall into the hands of "factions" (what we would call special interest groups) because, "They will use the power, when they have acquired it, to the purposes of gratifying their own interest and ambition, and it is scarcely possible, in very large republic, to call them to account for their misconduct, or to prevent their abuse of power."[39] Even a moment's glance at the current litany of scandals would make this quote seem prophetic. Once a far-removed and small group of people get unlimited power (through the *Necessary and Proper* and *Supremacy Clauses*) watch out!

This argument created the foundation of the political parties of the United States. Those that felt that the federal government should maintain complete supremacy through implied powers were the Federalists, while those that wanted a literal interpretation of the Constitution were called Republicans[40] The states' rights position was based on the Tenth Amendment and insisted that federal power could never expand beyond those enumerated in Article I, Section VIII. Many among the Republican ranks were those who opposed the idea of a new Constitution at all. They fought vehemently against ratification and committed

---

38   Idem

39   Idem

40   The name "Republican" confuses many students of history. This is mostly because it is logical to compare the name to today's Republican party. The party referenced here began as the Anti-Federalist party. But Jefferson realized that to actually win political power one needed to be "Pro" something. This led to the Democratic-Republican party, which first appeared in the 1796 campaign. The Republican party today began in 1854.

The American Revolution

themselves to keeping the new national regime as weak as possible.

But the public sentiment seems to have largely been to support the new system. The Federalists were able to win elections for both executive and legislative offices. George Washington as a national hero was able to rally the country's electorate to trust the nationalists to establish much of the federal powers, we are all familiar with today. Many in today's MAGA crowd tout the General's great contribution to our notions of liberty but forget that he was one of the earliest proponents of increasing the power of the central government. What made Washington unique was that he remained loyal to his "country" Virginia, which acted as a type of "self" control over Washington's propensity to increase his own authority. He was conscientious to include both Federalists and Anti-Federalists in his cabinet. He made decisions with the purpose of ensuring clear power for the federal government but tried to allay fears of tyranny by placing limits on certain legislation.[41] The cabinet meetings began to get very heated and eventually Jefferson left the government because he was losing too many arguments. Madison changed from his Federalist leanings when he witnessed the party playing too loose with the idea of expanding national power by mere "interpretation" instead of

---

41   The best example of this comes in the fight over the National Bank. Jefferson argued that the power to have a bank was not in the expressed powers and therefore unconstitutional, while Hamilton used the "necessary and proper" clause to say that the bank was indeed necessary and proper. Washington's decision was to create a national bank but with a 20-year charter so that there would be a "check" on the bank's power. If it proved to be tyrannical then the people could simply refuse to renew the charter.

Don De Angelo

following the proscribed method of amending the Constitution. He would remain a Republican for the rest of his political life.

It is not important to retell the entire narrative of American history, which is easily enough obtained. However, it becomes useful to be reminded of those critical moments to establish certain facts. The Republicans did not sit idly by for long. Beginning with Jefferson and Madison, we can see the establishment of anti-federal arguments, which are seen in current anti-government rhetoric.

The *Virginia and Kentucky Resolutions* introduced the idea of "Compact Theory" and "nullification," which has reared its head at various moments in American political history.[42] The main principle was the idea that the "United" States of America was in fact a union of sovereign states, who voluntarily gave up a certain amount of their sovereignty to a national government. This social contract (Constitution) spells out this relationship. Since the states were the founders of this new government, they were therefore the best judges of which acts were constitutional. Any state that found federal action in conflict with the Constitution was therefore at liberty to ignore its execution within its boundaries (hence nullification – zeroing out the effect of something).

James Madison's role lends credence to the work since he helped to write the Constitution. It appears on its surface to be "anti-federal" but has at its base is a desire to keep the Republican states tied to the national government. It was an attempt to curb the very specific actions of the administration of John

---

42   The VA and KY Resolutions were a response to the Alien and Sedition Acts passed by the Federalists during what was called the "Quasi War" with France. The Pro-French Republicans found themselves the victims of these acts and wanted the laws repealed and Federalists routed in the next election.

The American Revolution

Adams. However, the introduction of the idea of nullification proved poisonous to the Union.

Even the Federalists toyed with the ideas introduced by Jefferson and Madison. When the nation declared war on Great Britain in 1812, New Englanders were furious. Their trading relations with England were endangered and they had voted *en mass* against the conflict. When the Federalist states met to demand further limits to federal power, it was seen as treason. The result was the destruction of the Federalist party. The following "Era of Good Feelings" marked a period of national unity. It appears the idea of questioning federal power was dead.

The unity was short-lived. Arguments over tariff rates soon pitted southern and northern interests. While the Constitution clearly gives the sole power of imposing tariffs to the national government it was intended as the primary source of revenue. John C. Calhoun (at the time the Vice President) felt that the Constitution did not explicitly permit the federal government to impose tariffs for the purpose of protecting domestic industries. The result was the *South Carolina Exposition and Protest* (1828). In it, Calhoun revived the idea of nullification and hinted that secession might be a valid remedy for southern suffering under the "Tariff of Abomination."[43]

This argument began to fester and grow into southern intransigence regarding every issue important to the American people. Tariffs, internal improvements, and a national bank – all issues

---

43 Calhoun's theory culminated in an event called *The Nullification Crisis* in which South Carolina declared that the state would no longer collect the tariff. President Andrew Jackson, himself a "states-rights" advocate, imposed federal authority and promised to lead an army to SC to collect the tariff and hang Calhoun!

boiled down to federal vs. states' rights. The ultimate divider was slavery. Southerners used the state's rights argument to justify the unjustifiable – the unthinkable. The only way to end this argument was unfortunately the Civil War and the death of over 700,000 Americans. Even after the war, southerners refused to accept the notion of black *citizens* and the end to compact theory. The result were *Jim Crow* laws meant to undermine federal acts to aid former slaves and integrate blacks into society in general.

The pains of civil war and the frustrations of Reconstruction, led many in America to distrust the whole idea of state "power." In this era, the assumption began to develop that states could not be trusted and only the federal government could ensure liberty for all citizens. Americans stopped using the word "union" to describe the country and began to use "nation" instead. Today we say the United States IS, when before the Civil War it was common to say, the United States ARE.

The prowess of the states was further drawn into question during the Progressive Era. Many Americans were suffering abuses – either in the home, the workplace, or the civic arena. To the progressives, the federal government could and should be the active partner in solving these social ills. While it is admirable that progressives used the amendment process for their main objectives, it is still remarkable to witness the onslaught of legislation creating new federal departments and additional power for national regulation.

The main tool for this was the expressed power of the federal government to regulate inter-state commerce. By stretching the meaning of exactly what that meant, the progressives were able to expand government power without the constraint of the

The American Revolution

Tenth Amendment or the need to get state approval[44]. Because it was seen at the time as a positive good and a "limited" expansion of commercial regulation, there seemed to be a broad consensus.

The final nail in the states' rights coffin came with the New Deal of the 1930s. Here the states were in fact falling to pieces. Their collective and/or singular inability to solve the economic suffering of the American people caused everyone to look for salvation from the federal government. The FDR administration started its expansion of federal power with the Bank Holiday of 1933. Within the next ten years the power of the national government would expand beyond even the dreams of progressives two decades earlier. Although giving the entire economic policy over to the national government did little to correct the nation's economic woes, the fact that most Americans perceived a regime that "cared" made the policies feel like they worked.[45]

The result has been a mythological status for the idea of federal power and the notion that an individual's prosperity is dependent on the actions of government. This Keynesian version of government became part of the post-war (World War II) consensus that underscored the idea that it was now a main part of the

---

44   This is a reference to the "Necessary and Proper" clause, or what is today referred to as the "Elastic" clause. It is at the end of Article I, Section VIII. This states that in order to do its job under the Constitution, government is given all the power it needs. This clause has given the government the ability to expand its power without having to either justify it under strict construction or amending the document.

45   It is instructive to read more current literature about the New Deal and FDR. For years, it was nearly impossible to find anyone to second guess the policies of Roosevelt and the expansion of federal power. Amity Schlaes has written a magnificent book, *The Forgotten Man* and Burton Folsom has written *New Deal, Raw Deal.* These are excellent contrary looks at the period.

Don De Angelo

government's mandate to ensure full employment and economic stability. For the next thirty years, it was almost treasonous to suggest anything different.

That security lasted until Ronald Reagan was able to get elected by questioning the idea that national government was a positive good. With his infamous quote that, "government is not the solution, it is the problem," Reagan smashed through the museum case of progressive idealism. However, by that time the nationalist ideals of a strong central power and cradle-to-grave protectionism was considered sacrosanct. Thousands of Americans, particularly unionized workers and various interest groups were dependent on the largess of the federal regime. To suggest a smaller federal government was to jeopardize numerous constituencies accustomed to their share of federal spending.

While the "Reagan Revolution" did set the stage for future trimming of government budgets, the relative size of national institutions remained intact. Reagan's sweeping tax cuts were revisited later and were hiked on higher earners. The massive defense build-up was a conservative Keynesian program since all of it was on borrowed money. The dilemma for conservatives was figuring out how to sell the ideals of smaller government while imposing a federal remedy on the states. There was irony in the notion that states had to be convinced that they should take on more governing responsibility to exercise sovereign power. The Republicans now found themselves in control of a regime they wanted to destroy.

The added problem for conservative Republicans was that they wanted to curb federal power but also wanted to impose new national mandates regarding various social issues, namely abortion and traditional understandings of marriage. The

The American Revolution

"neo-conservative" idea of imposing on the states what they could or could not do regarding social norms ran counter to their ideals of a limited, federal government. George W. Bush's *progressive conservative* administration proved the ultimate disappointment for traditional conservatives hoping for further dismantling of the federal government.

The confusion permitted an articulate and attractive candidate to offer both. Barack Obama ran on a platform that promised "efficient" government for those tired of growing federal waste and a tax cut for 95% of Americans to reassure those dependent on big government without any personal sacrifices. Amid yet another economic disaster it seemed like a dream come true. It turned out to only be a dream.

When the hyper-Keynesian program of the Obama administration proved just short of a disaster, those who were already prone to fear central authority took to the streets. The "Tea Party" of 2009 was a revival of anti-federalist rhetoric. It is as though we have come full circle. Their anger and frustration propelled a new class of politician whose first response to any government action is to say "No!" Obama's unwillingness to compromise with this new expression of small government created the standoff that continues in current policy debates.

The reality of a possible and permanent shrinking of the federal government's spending has begun to sink into those Americans most dependent upon it. The "Occupy Wall Street" movement was at its base a nationalist movement. It insisted that not only should the power of the federal government remain but should grow. Any concern for the national solvency should be secondary to the comfort of these constituencies. While the movement has failed to articulate a clear set of demands, it was a struggle

Don De Angelo

between those who see government as the main obstacle to their individual happiness and those who feel the government is the only guarantor of their prosperity. This is the moment when Marxist ideology really became a viable worldview to espouse, particularly in the Democratic party.

To all this one must ask – where will the new "balance of power" rest? The neo-nationalists seem to prefer federal power for the sake of *equity* and the neo-antifederalists are crying out for dispersed powers for the sake of "liberty." The clincher is that neither party's platform completely answers these demands. Those same Tea Party activists are with MAGA Republicans until the party begins to add conservative moral imperatives and the Occupy Wall Street crowds lean towards Democrats until they hear about bailouts for banks and large government institutions. Is it time for a third party if not multiple parties?

The election of 2016 was the guttural expression of both extremes. The Democratic party engaged in a tug-of-war over just how much Marxist ideology should be incorporated into the party's platform. Essentially, Bernie Sanders' campaign was the culmination of the socialist activism of the 1960s and 1970s. His *millennial* support came from young adults who were frustrated by the reality that making it in the real world is actually very difficult. They want "Free" tuition and their student loans forgiven. They want to have "Free" health care and subsidized housing so they can afford to buy an actual house (none of this silly "starter" home or condo). And this all must be done in a way that will not increase our carbon footprint. No discussion of whether any of this is constitutional or even how we will ever be able to pay the bill. The younger generations who have been raised to believe that there should never be any obstacles in their way or there is

The American Revolution

evil afoot, cannot fathom a government that won't "care" about making their lives easier.

The Republican party devolved into what can only be described as a political and personal food fight. Donald Trump was able to take a party based on tough talk down a road so low that it made a very crude American population cringe. There was very little debate on issues. But Trump was able to tap into another odd narrative. Those disgruntled WASP-based voters who feel their country is becoming a foreign place to them, saw Trump as a person who would "drain the swamp." It is not racist. But it is classical nationalism, which can feed on racial fears and turn a country into a Balkanized war zone.

What should have been the real story during the campaign turned out to be a joke – Libertarian party candidate Gary Johnson. The Libertarian party had the best opportunity to make a difference as a third party. The platform called for the maximum amount of personal liberty with a smaller central government. The party incorporates the original philosophy of our nation's founders that would solve a great deal of the nation's problems. But a media that embraces Marxist ideology was never going to be open to classical liberal party. Gary Johnson himself proved not ready for prime time – "Aleppo" – need I say more? In an election cycle where more than 30% of the voters hated both major candidates, a third option should have been wildly popular.

The result, a media -- convinced that the people are malleable and stupid – were completely wrong. Americans in California are convinced that socialism is the way to go; but apparently, few other states were ready to play ball. The invested media became determined to bring down a president and especially a president

Don De Angelo

who thinks he is the second coming! Messianic complexes are very difficult to bear, but when the president *and* the media both feel, they are destined to save the world the very fabric of American society is challenged.

The media was wrong in 2016 because they openly backed a deeply flawed candidate, tried to belittle any challengers, and discourage conservative voters, and then acted hurt and shocked when their candidate lost. The worst part is that they are incapable of getting over it. Donald Trump seems to understand that millions of Americans are fed up with a central government determined to take over every aspect of their lives and doing so in the most ineffective and inefficient means possible. Every attack on Trump increases his appeal among those who feel ignored.

Now, we see states run by Democrats who in theory believe that the federal government should have dominant power, suing the federal government for trampling on state power. California spent millions of tax dollars trying to sue the Trump administration over authority the constitution says are *only* federal power – such as immigration. Imagine if a Republican state like Alabama were to create sanctuary cities that nullified civil rights laws; and yet, we have places in the United States where government officials are openly refusing to enforce federal laws. Democrats behaving like Republicans and vice versa is not a sign of coming together. Nor is it an indication of ideological superiority. It is a sign that neither party really cares about their philosophical purity but rather simply to maintain their own hold on power.

When this happens then there is no balance of power. There is only power by a duopoly of elites who will do or say anything to keep their seat at the trough. They were able to distribute over

The American Revolution

$4.75 *trillion* every year since 2010 and will not relinquish their share without a major rebuke by the American people.

Regardless of what the media and cultural elites might say, most people are very well in tune with what they want out of their government. They may not always have the SAT-word vocabulary to articulate it; but they certainly know when they are being scammed. Lazy thinking gets all of us in trouble because we miss key facts that would change our calculation(s). That is not stupidity – it is the normal outcome when people have busy lives and multiple responsibilities. That should not be a green light for politicians and media personalities to treat citizens as dupes or pushovers.

The Current Reality

The odd thing about the two main movements – Tea Party and Occupy Wall Street (OWS) – is that there are some common areas of agreement. Both groups resent the federal government bailing out Wall Street banks while ignoring the plight of the average American. Were the federal government simply to have given each unemployed person a check for $30,000, the price tag would have been a mere $420 billion. That's a savings for $380 billion over the cost of the bailouts (minimum). If the government could afford to rebuild every road in America the process would take about a year and employ half the 14 million unemployed, who would again be unemployed whenever such projects ended. The dilemma with this idea is that it would establish a new standard of government – paying people to not work, which is what occurred during the COVID pandemic.

Don De Angelo

Where they disagree is who to blame. Tea Party people blame the government while the OWS blame the billionaires and their heartless greed. The reality is that they are both correct!

Many rich people are greedy and have absolutely no regard for the consequences for their conspicuous consumption. Corporate executive compensation is inexplicably too high and disproportionate to their actual contribution to business growth and increased economic value. Corporations have a very strong influence over the federal government because they can "buy" access in ways the average citizen cannot. Look at the names of those in the federal departments dealing with the nation's economy and you will see many of the names that were formerly on the board of the country's major multinationals, especially investment houses. If corporations were to function as truly free market enterprises, no CEO would garner such high salaries without shouldering incredible liability. In a world where companies know they will be bailed out because it was government intrusions that encourage their bad behavior; CEOs can negotiate such ridiculous *golden parachutes*.

However, is this influence because of corporate intrusion into government or government involvement in business practices? It is an interesting puzzle. Since the early 1900s we have seen the federal government take a greater and greater role in the daily operations of business in America. Excluding anti-trust laws that prevent monopoly behavior, there seems to be an odd reality that large corporations have increased ever since we have concentrated economic authority in Washington. Is the current action by business the result of corporate greed or the natural tendency to concentrate influence wherever there is concentrated power? Rent-seeking corporations will help draft complex regulations

The American Revolution

to keep out competition. The government becomes a gatekeeper and not a watch dog for the public.

The financial crisis of 2007 may prove the point. Since the 1930s more and more banking regulation has been taken on by the federal government. The result has been the consolidation of most of the country's banks. These large lending institutions have been slow in responding to the credit needs of many Americans – namely those with lower incomes.

To respond to this seeming disregard for these under-represented groups, the federal government created Fannie Mae and Freddie Mac and institutions that would regulate the extension of credit. Both Republican and Democratic administrations found it popular to encourage Fannie and Freddie to promote home ownership to lower income families. Republicans saw it to make minorities and the poor more "stake holders" in the American economy. Democrats saw it as a means of leveling the playing field and providing equal access to the "American Dream."

When property prices began to rise in the 1990s the government continued to encourage more lending to lower income people for buying homes. This was done when all signs were that prices might be moving above the average American's ability to pay. There are easily obtained You Tube videos of Senator Christopher Dodd (CT) and Representative Barney Frank (MA) as late as 2006 claiming there was no market bubble, and that Freddie and Fannie must keep encouraging more lending.

Bankers began joking about how these were called NINJA loans – No Income, No Job, or Assets! Everyone in the know could see there was a problem but if the government was saying, "lend, lend!" they were more than happy to play ball. To hedge their bets banks began to package these loans into assets they sold to investors who were also reading government assurances about the value of home prices. Then these same banks began an "insurance" program called derivatives. This legal Ponzi scheme was a desperate act to make a shaky market a cash cow for anyone who had the stomach to play. The rest of the story you may already know.

When it came crumbling down the American people turned to their government for help. They wanted their savings and investments protected against a complete collapse and the response was the bailout program under George W. Bush. The Treasury Asset Recovery Program (TARP) was further expanded by Barack Obama. The immediate crisis supposedly averted, Americans turned their attentions to their jobs and personal credit.

The government had to bail out the big banks and investors because it was their prodding, and easy credit rates that made the crisis. So, the politicians gave the banks billions of dollars and then told them that there would be much stricter rules on how they lend money and that the banks would be held accountable for every dollar "loaned" to them. Suddenly, the federal government wanted conservative lending standards and the sub-market lenders virtually disappeared. The natural reaction was to stop lending money to most borrowers to ensure that the banks stayed solvent. The banks really could not win. If they kept lending the government would accuse them of continuing the irresponsible behavior that led to the financial collapse. If they hoarded their money, they were accused of greed. All this behavior was created by a government that was trying to micromanage the economy to fulfill non-economic objectives, such as fairness in the housing market and equal access to capital. The fact that most financial officials in the government are former executives of major

The American Revolution

finance corporations regulated by the government give credence to suspicions of collusion.

The resulting recession gives both parties something to complain about. Democrats can rightfully point to the banks and their predominantly Republican supporters to over-speculation and greed. Republicans can equally point to the shameless politicization of the financial industry by Democrats trying to manipulate the economy to please their own constituencies. Sorting through the facts gets us all to some very important realities.

The first thing that needs to be accepted is that everyone allowed themselves to be foolish. For as long as we have been an industrialized nation, economic cycles have existed. They follow a pattern of boom-and-bust periods that seem to come every 20 to 40 years. The idea that no one saw it coming is silly. Low interest rates at a time of 4% unemployment were unthinkable in almost any economic theory and yet the Federal Reserve Board made sure that rates stayed well below what the market could handle. Easy money and a government essentially demanding banks make more loans was a recipe for disaster and we all knew it.

There are millions of Americans who thought the home they were buying was too good to be true – they were right. For them to complain that the nasty bank people forced them into a loan *they* knew they couldn't afford is laughable. We all played the game in some respect, and we paid the price.

The second important thing to grasp is the spending spree governments have been on since the 1930s. The idea that this country is suffering from a lack of revenue is a falsehood given the amount of money collected in the various taxes, fees, and excises. Spending has simply outpaced revenue. The deficit under

Don De Angelo

George Bush, which Democrats decried as a travesty, was about $161 billion. In 2010 that deficit rose to $1.3 trillion and has continued around that figure every year. Soaking the rich will never make that up. This is a complete failure of fiscal discipline. When the economy was booming, the government should have been weaning the American people away from government largess. Donald Trump's brag that he had the greatest economy since 1969 is meaningless if it did not result in budget surpluses and diminished government programs. It also would not have hurt to set some money aside for a rainy day. Nations with sovereign wealth funds tend not to suffer in economic downturns.[46]

George W. Bush told us we could fight two wars, cut taxes and all still go shopping. Had he called the nation to collective sacrifice when he stood at Ground Zero and asked us all to chip in, it would most likely have happened. The rich whose children were the least likely to be the ones sent into battle could have been convinced to give back a little bit in taxes to finance the conflict. There may have been a willingness to put a 10-cent tax on gasoline. Regardless of the political risks involved, Bush missed an opportunity to accomplish national security without damaging our financial solvency. His neo-con agenda of nation-building was a detour from the narrowly defined rationale of responding to an attack on the United States. While few would argue against making the Taliban of Afghanistan pay for what happened on 9/11; trying to bring democracy to the Middle East was most certainly not a national priority and Biden's *exit strategy* was a

---

46 https://www.thebalance.com/us-deficit-by-year-3306306 Current debt is about $22 Trillion.

The American Revolution

fiasco. We have long passed one trillion dollars and thousands of ruined lives with little to show for our sacrifices.

Let us not make any mistake. The Democrats seemed in lock step with the Republicans. In their obsession to appear just as patriotic as conservatives, the liberals signed on to these wars with little to no resistance. The nation entered another massive growth spurt. Both parties wanted to keep the banquet table full so that the voters would remain confident in their government. And the people continued to gorge themselves without regard to their long-term health or security.

President Obama spent nearly $9 trillion dollars in borrowed money trying to fix the economy using tired Keynesian models. The problem is that the situation today is nothing like that of the 1930s of which Mr. Obama waxed so nostalgic. First, the nation does not have the capital reserves of the treasury under FDR. While the debt-to-GDP figures might be similar, the fact that the United States in 1932 stood as the largest creditor nation with an intact industrial complex provided considerable cushion for government activism.[47]

Secondly, FDRs jobs programs came at a time without unemployment insurance. Without a government job, many would go without any income at all. Today, the government has extended unemployment benefits to 99 weeks (with further extensions to come). If you are a laid off banker and you could continue collecting benefits, would you really except a job paving America's roads? One could argue that this simply defies reason. It is also

---

47   https://www.forbes.com/sites/peterferrara/2012/07/12/obamanom
ics-the-final-nail-in-the-discredited-keynesian-coffin/#61c55145ba7d See Also
https://www.thebalance.com/us-deficit-by-year-3306306

Don De Angelo

important to accept that most people are rational. If they get a temporary government job under a stimulus plan, they know that the project will someday end. Those working under such conditions do not behave like a typical consumer, choosing instead to pay off debt or save money for possible setbacks. Neither is a dependable spark for economic growth.

Finally, the projects in question needed environmental studies, labor union negotiations, and state government cooperation. None of this was considered before the dollars were allocated and the result was the president's now infamous quip, "some of those shovel ready projects have proven to be not so shovel ready". The remedy of course is to start a new Keynesian spending program – right? The COVID pandemic put the entire world into this model of governance, and we saw neither fiscal discipline nor competent policy. Billions of people suffered all over the world because of these choices.

The dilemma for the United States is that we need a fundamental shift in how the government(s) operates without sparking another economic downturn. This is difficult because if economic growth is stifled the electorate takes it out on the party in power (in this case the Democrats). If the economic stalemate is perceived as a political stunt to gain power, the Republicans will suffer. No one wants to make the first move in a game where every player will most likely lose in the short run.

How does an evenly divided Congress get itself together and begin the process and avoid taking blame for the outcome? You appoint a special commission, in this case a "Super Committee" to come up with a formula and drop-dead date for completion. One essentially knows that it is all doomed to failure, but one keeps the pressure on these lucky 24 politicians to fall on their

The American Revolution

swords for the good of their respective parties. And that is exactly what was done. The Simpson-Bowles Commission has submitted its findings and recommendations many years ago now.[48]

President Biden has adapted the World Economic Forum's *Great Reset* as his own *Build Back Better*. The administration seems to have chosen to remove him from the process and instead have him travel the United States blaming everyone and everything else. His hope is that this will deflect blame from his own failed policies but forgets that his own party controls *the* most powerful seat in the Congress – Senate Majority Leader, Chuck Schumer (NY). The Majority Leader can ignore bills if so chooses and can make it impossible for budgets to ever see the Senate floor. If Republican house bills die in the Senate, the president can say he is doing all he can and continue to govern by executive orders and emergency spending measures. It may be good politics, but it is a long-term nightmare for the stability of the country.

Every American from the President of the United States to the soon-to-be first voters need to understand that sacrifice will mean something real this time. Those of us who for whatever reason have come to depend on government subsidies or other handouts, will need to see those benefits go away. Those my age or younger (under 60) will need to accept stricter rules on entitlements. The military will have to be reformed in ways that mean a leaner fighting force that might not be able to answer every call for help around the world. This is the beginning of a

---

48 https://www.thebalance.com/simpson-bowles-plan-summary-history-would-it-work-3306323. No one is serious about controlling federal spending.

long and difficult process that will in the end pay out very big dividends.

The most important thing to remember is that any political system has its darker side. The devolved government of conservatives comes at the expense of those who will not or cannot do for themselves. Compassion is not a government attribute – it can attempt to be fair and arbitrate between invested parties – government welfare is a payoff to the poor to keep them compliant in a free market system with inherent winners and losers. It is the foundation of all socialist government to mitigate the harsh reality of failure within real economic competition. It is a form of retribution. It is not compassion. So, for the small government activist there must be a lower level or collective response to the plight of the poor and disempowered. To say it will fall to private charity is playing light with the realities of dynamic economies – some people will be lost in the shuffle and that spells genuine and unacceptable suffering.

The nationalist economics agenda prescribed by mainstream Democrats also needs to come clean with the darker side of its own. As one centralizes more power and authority it will invite more influence peddling and corruption. At some point, you raise taxes too high and still do not have enough money to support all the great things being done for the country. Regulations and fiscal burdens begin to push enterprises out of the marketplace leaving only the larger players who can afford the lobbying necessary to land large government contracts, which become the only way to stay profitable. If the tax base gets in any way diminished, you face the fate of Greece. This may seem trivial given the size of Greece in the grander scheme of the international economy, especially given the reality that there are

The American Revolution

many nations around to bail them out. But who will be there to bail us out?

A Broad Blueprint

What does the nation need to do? The issues have been debated by many, so I do not necessarily offer new remedies. It is essential though to be reminded that it is time to give these ideas a new sense of urgency as we face a growing debt and a stagnant economy.

The proper Size of Government

It is time to make permanent changes to the reach of the federal government. It is also important to consider every program even those that are considered sacred cows. Should the federal government be involved in welfare, education, or agricultural research? Do we need a federal OSHA and state-level offices? How do we make the federal government stay within those powers expressly given in Article I, Section VIII? The material might seem parochial but without answering these questions we fall into the same trap that has snared the Bowles-Simpson commission. The optimal standard is to keep the SHEW business at the local or state level.

The nation should come to the same conclusion Madison arrived at in 1816. Having been a long-time states' rights advocate for over 20 years, the president was hoping to complete the Jeffersonian dream of a weakened federal government and thriving

Don De Angelo

states. The War of 1812 changed all of that. The absence of the Bank of the United States (BUS) left the federal government without the needed funds to fight the British. Depending on state banks for the money proved difficult because the largest banks were in states that did not support the war and were reluctant to cooperate. Depending on state militias also proved a disaster. Madison was also confronted by his long-time aversion to federally funded public works. Moving the army and military supplies without sufficient roads was embarrassing.

In the euphoria of the victory in 1815, Henry Clay of Kentucky introduced a new program for national development – The American System. This legislation addressed all the shortcomings that confronted the government during the war. Madison too became convinced that his resistance to federal power had to go. Madison's rationale has become my own. If Article I, Section VIII lists the power as being indeed an expressed federal power, then how the federal government handles it is a question for the Congress. The state governments had their say through their appointed Senators. This is something present states do not have because of the Seventeenth Amendment. He signed the bill for a second Bank of the United States. He signed a new "protective" tariff in 1816. Even in the bill he vetoed – a proposal to pay for internal improvements – was not a rejection of the expansion of federal power. What Madison wanted was an amendment to give the federal government the "expressed" power to pay for public works projects, which cross state boundaries.

That has been a revelation to me. It seems easy to look at the Constitution and say, "what's listed here as a federal power, should only be a federal power." I don't need to fight this power. But if the federal government tries to expand into other territory,

The American Revolution

then the only right thing to do is to amend the Constitution or deny the federal government's intrusion.

So, what does this say about "size?"

The federal government has placed itself in the middle of projects and programs that were not listed as federal power. Most of what we are now facing in terms of debt and partisan griping comes from this condition. With every new program started by the federal government new constituencies are created. These voters then grab the attention of legislators who support the respective program and create new bureaucracies whose very livelihood depends on sustaining such programs. This "Iron Triangle" becomes accustomed to the government's largess and take the funding for granted. Soon any discussion about cutting the program becomes a turf war between the parties. Whether it is a multinational corporation getting federal assistance to market their products overseas or agricultural researchers studying the mating habits of the Mediterranean Fruit Fly, every dollar spent has a voter attached. Threaten the program and these people become animated.

This is particularly true of public employee-unions, whose very livelihood depends on government spending. Whenever you even think of ending a program, union executives put their members into action. These are everyday workers who are now in danger of losing their careers. This makes for bad images on television. How does any fair-minded American look into the face of one of these workers feel good about shutting down any part of the government? Did you watch the demonstrations in

Don De Angelo

Wisconsin and Ohio and think, "these poor people really are getting screwed?" At first, I did. Then I began to think about what was really going on. These employees were essentially saying that they want the taxpayers to underwrite their further employment regardless of the cost. The average public employee is making significantly more than the average taxpayer, and this is simply an unsustainable formula. Franklin Roosevelt – the champion of the modern labor agenda – never wanted public employees to be unionized.

Reading the Preamble of the Constitution can be rather instructive: "We the People of the United States, in order to form a more perfect Union, establish Justice, insure [sic] domestic Tranquility, provide for the common defense, promote the general Welfare, and secure the Blessings of Liberty to ourselves and our Posterity, do ordain and establish this Constitution for the United States of America." I see five roles for the federal regime: Justice, Domestic Tranquility (security), defense, general welfare (creating stable economic environments), and liberty (individual and collective freedoms). Imagine the federal government with only five departments and not fifteen.

Justice is truly important at a federal level because the process of law should be uniform throughout the nation. Permit the states to do their own thing – like we did on segregation in the South – and citizens are no longer ensured that their freedoms are secured. This is also true of liberty. Their needs to be a federal standard for our rights and liberties so that no matter where we go, we are guaranteed equal treatment. This is why the Fourteenth Amendment is so very critical. Domestic tranquility was really about security. Shays Rebellion scared a lot of people in 1786. Insurrectionists threatened the Massachusetts government

The American Revolution

and came close to spreading throughout the region. James Madison realized that their needed to be some national force to make sure this could not happen again. Common defense seems straightforward enough – we need a military to defend our borders and repel threats to the country. General welfare is a tricky one because what constitutes "general"? In my estimation, this should mean that the federal government should ensure a stable currency, a well-regulated work environment and a uniform set of standards and practices to promote the economic growth of the nation.

Notice that the word education does not exist, nor does energy or agriculture or a large list of current federal programs. There may have been perfectly legitimate reasons to have the federal government intervene in these and other areas, but it never made much fiscal sense and has created a national regime that has become "too big to fail." And, so we sit by as Democrats and Republicans duke it out over who gets to have their pet programs alive and still not appear to be a heartless bastard. It's no wonder they can't do their job.

Let's make some cuts!

Begin with the truly frivolous. There is simply no need for the government to be in the Arts and Humanities business. The NEA and NEH should be cut off. It may be possible to give each institution a one-time, billion-dollar endowment to keep them afloat, but the relationship ends there. If art or social science work cannot find funding within the private sector or universities then maybe it just shouldn't be done. Goodbye to federally

Don De Angelo

subsidized marketing for American products overseas. If corporations cannot afford to promote their own products, then they have no business trying to sell overseas. We can also get ahead of the game by ending crop subsidies – especially for crops that are grown to make biofuels.

There is so much that doesn't make sense and yet these programs continue. Did you know that we still have a Bureau of Indian Affairs (BIA)? It seems repulsive that the United States still considers Indians as needing to be managed by the government. I would kill the BIA and turn over all national parks and preserves to those tribes we took the land from in the first place. That way we stop paying taxes to "manage" Indians and give these tribes additional sources of revenue. The remaining federal lands should be surrendered to the states. This will also allow us to cut the national parks service and most of the Department of the Interior.

So long to the Department of Housing and Urban Development – we can give away the existing federal housing to current occupants -- call it an Urban Homestead Act-- and shut down the whole thing. If cities require federal assistance to stay viable then they should just disappear. Not kidding. If the federal government ever has surplus money and wants to help the states, the best way would be to give block grants of money to the states and county governments and let them handle their own problems as they see fit. Stop all these separate programs with their specific goals and mandates and instead allow lower governments, which are closer to the people, determine where best to apply resources.

The government needs to sell the Tennessee Valley Authority to private enterprise. Why is the federal government involved

The American Revolution

with distribution of electricity? I'd rather see the government set that money aside for possible emergency power failures that seem to cripple parts of this country from time to time. This should also happen to Amtrak, NASA and the US Postal Service.

The president has recently promoted the idea of combining all agencies related to economic interests to be consolidated into one department. This is a great idea but lacks a specific formula for long-term reduction in federal power and is most likely an election year ploy to appear as though Obama is committed to efficient government ("Trust me with your increasing tax dollars because I will spend it all with great frugality"). I would go further. One federal program for any one task – eliminate any duplicity.

Imagine This Framework

Department of Foreign Affairs (DOFA): Deals with all diplomacy, trade, and foreign intelligence. Make this the primary focus of our global interactions. Less use of military assets and more focus on economic relations and alliance formation.

Department of Domestic Affairs (DODA): Manages all internal issues of infrastructure and safety concerns such as TSA, FAA and National Transportation and Safety Administration.

Department of Interstate Commerce (DISCO): The big change is the limitation of federal regulation to publicly traded stock companies and corporations issuing public bonds. Private, small companies will be regulated by the states where they are based. The FTC and SEC would be in this department.

Don De Angelo

Department of the Treasury (DOT): Another major reform would be the elimination of the Federal Reserve. There would be an Open Market Committee to advise the treasury on currency valuation and supply, but the government will need to take direct responsibility of the financial markets. No more quantitative easing. If there must be debt, it will be sold on the open market. Budgets will be made by the Congress and the DOT will have the Office of Management and Budget to advise the president on how to execute it.

Department of Defense (DOD): This is about the same except we add the border patrol to their duties. The CIA will disappear in this scenario so military intelligence will be beefing up.

Department of Justice (DOJ): After a complete review of all the abuses in this department, and the removal of upper management, this department will look familiar. The FBI will either be radically reduced in power or disappear. Federal police powers will be given to federal marshals who can add investigative powers if needed.

Everything else would be on the chopping block. This is a dramatic oversimplification but think of the savings in annual budgets! This also assumes other tasks (not listed in the Expressed powers) would be taken on by either the states or local governments. Five departments doing what the Constitution expressly proscribes would allow for the government to become expert at what it does and demand that the people become more self-sufficient. The amount of taxes required would diminish significantly and the budget deficit would evaporate. This model would lead to massive layoffs of unionized employees and leave many Americans without services.

The American Revolution

Beginning to see the problem?

This is just the beginning of a long list of unnecessary spending, and yet each one of the above has dependents. Were it known that these and other departments were under this kind of threat there would be riots in the streets to put BLM and Antifa to shame. Trusting politicians to hammer out these reforms may be asking too much. I don't know that these could ever be done but the difference it would make on America's finances and political corruption is immeasurable. The departments marked for demise each have public employee unions and constituents that would demonstrate in the streets and sue in the federal courts. Many of the U.S. judges are liberal enough that they would place injunctions on many of these efforts. Public opinion might first react to the impending layoffs rather than the lasting financial benefits.

Taxation

So here we are – a new way of looking at the federal government without eliminating the powers enumerated in the Constitution. There remain two problems: how to ensure financial support to the lower levels of government and how to distribute representation to keep watch on possible federal overreach. This is important because we are prescribing additional power to the states, which will require more revenue. There is also a genuine fear that over time the federal government will use the *Elastic Clause* to expand its authority.

<u>*Federal taxes:*</u> The taxes collected at the federal level should be clear, even, and consistent. The best solution is to have all the states give up their sales taxes and make that the exclusive

148

Don De Angelo

revenue stream of the federal government. This would provide a single sales tax rate for the entire country. It would also allow for the taxation of e-commerce and imported products. There may be a need to exempt medical categories and unprocessed food, but a 10% tax would be hidden in the price of the product (how nice to go to the register and pay what is on the tag!) and garner over $3 trillion. The tax should be placed on all imported goods. This tax system would level the playing field among the states and permit the treasury to earn money every time there is an economic transaction. Do not repeal the Sixteenth Amendment because the U.S. government might find itself in a true emergency (war, depression, or natural disaster) and need additional revenues. It might also be popular and useful at some point to ask the very wealthy to pay a low, flat tax to pay down the national debt. Eliminate the IRS and watch the free market explode with growth.

There should also be permission for the federal government to continue with any fees, surcharges and excises collected. These are still intrusions into most Americans' lives and should be earmarked for specific programs (i.e., gasoline taxes to pay for the interstate freeways). The states should also continue to collect these funds as so long as these are handled as *user fees* and not as slush funds for aimless government spending.

State Taxes: Bigger states, such as California have a different reality than most. Most states could probably exist on a flat 10% income tax. No deductions, no exemptions, or deletions and again no tax returns! Eliminate sales taxes and most excise taxes. Collecting a gas tax should be solely to finance state highway maintenance. Royalties for resource extraction should be invested in sovereign wealth funds to create financial stability for the

The American Revolution

state. Rainy Day funds are accounting schemes meant to make taxpayers feel better about how government spends their money. Sovereign wealth funds demonstrate a serious commitment to the financial and fiscal well-being of the people.

Bigger states should try to function by giving more power to their local governments for those day-to-day needs (the SHEW) of the people. By focusing on justice, infrastructure and higher education, large states could rely on flat taxes for the base of revenue and then use fees and excise taxes to pay for earmarked services. Get rid of property and inheritance taxes. The benefit here is to make government spending more accountable. If the state of California takes it's 5% and then San Francisco County takes another 5%, all should be well. If the people of San Francisco want to live in a Marxist *utopia*, then let them impose another 10% flat tax. In this system the real cost of more government becomes clear, and voters will live under the system they chose.

County (local) Taxes: When we go about our daily lives, we worry about having enough cops on the street, that garbage gets picked-up and that the schools are well funded. We want good health care and clear roads to drive on. These are local concerns and should be handled at the local level. Therefore, it is necessary to grant the most tax power to the local government. My preference is for county government over city regimes. This is mainly because it seems the most logical given the expansiveness of urban agendas and the historical propensity of city governments to be dominated by individual "dynasties."

In large states, such as California, this means that the income tax is best placed at this level. It should be flat, fair, and predictable. The flat 10% tax is great here. In this scenario, most government services would be done at this level.

150

Don De Angelo

Smaller states, such as Delaware, handles everything at the state level and cities doing very little. This is logical so every state should find its own balance. Eliminating duplication and waste should be the primary focus of the reform(s). And, whenever a service or agency can be eliminated, do it![49]

Representation

The states will need a safeguard for their reestablished powers. The expansion of federal power has come mostly through the loose interpretation of the expressed power to regulate interstate commerce. The original Constitution provided the best device to check that trend – the Senate. Before 1913, Senators were appointed by the state legislatures. This ensured that at least one house of the Congress would be mindful of state concerns regarding new legislation. The progressives felt that the Senate had become an elitist institution loaded with millionaires interested in lining their own pockets – and they were right. The Seventeenth Amendment placed Senators under the direct vote of the people – and look at our Senate today with its millionaires beholden to interest groups instead of the states they represent.

Repealing the Seventeenth Amendment would restore the original intent of the body – ensure that states have a direct say

---

49 It would be powerful to see the county government handling: Public Education (K-Community College/vocational school); Public Safety (fire, police, EMT); Public Health, and Public Welfare. The county legislatures would become very powerful and need public due diligence but the opportunity to really make a difference in one's daily life would be extraordinary. Smaller republics are more responsive and more democratic.

The American Revolution

in legislative outcomes. This would also give more weight to state elections, as the party with a majority of seats in the state legislature would influence who served. This would in turn call for more local media coverage, which might frustrate media consolidation under corporate controls.

Enough Already!

Harbor no delusions. Many, if not all the ideas may have been suggested before. They are not part of some grand manifesto or a panacea for the nation's ills. They are meant as a springboard to broader dialogue about the future structure of the United States' government. It is also not meant to force a particular ideology onto the American voter as much as to remind each voter of their obligation to think long and hard about their choices, and just how much power they want to grant to government.

Federal Welfare

Welfare, in its broadest context, means a whole host of issues that affect the wellbeing of those less fortunate among us. We cannot deal with welfare and not deal with drug addiction, mental health issues, and how we fund programs for poverty. The confrontation of these has created a booming career for hundreds of thousands of public employees – most of whom are unionized. The public employee unions, such as AFSME and SEIU, have enormous political clout as they raise millions of dollars and provide hundreds of volunteers for political campaigns. While

Don De Angelo

most media attention goes to interest groups like the NRA, these unions have a massively disproportional influence on what happens in government.

The first issue that must be addressed is the nation's drug addiction. It is always important to begin any discussion of narcotics requires an embrace of certain truths. First, we are a society obsessed with drugs. We pop pills, we drink incredible amounts of alcohol, and many are currently hysterical about legalizing marijuana. This is not a healthy approach to life and the escapism underlying all this behavior would require a separate book. Were the American people to find alternative vehicles for their relief, we would all be better off.

That having been said, there is nothing inherently wrong with occasional use of those thing that provide a "release" of some of the very real pressures of modern life. More importantly, it could be very strongly argued whether the federal government has any vested interest in the matter. The US War of Drugs has been a 40-year battle against the American people, and one could argue as to whether there could be any measurable improvement in handling drugs as an epidemic. Are we really helping people with addiction problems? We spend multiple billions of dollars every year to stop the supply of drugs, which make for great television when the Coast Guard makes the occasional bust. However, untold multitudes of users have been pushed into the dark corners of our communities and are forced into lives of crime and poverty.

Ending the drug war would help several issues. The federal government could simply cut this funding and ease budgetary burdens. The states could spend a fraction of their current budgets on law enforcement and focus solely on recovery and

The American Revolution

rehabilitation. Multiple recovering addicts will no longer have to face the obstacles of reforming their lives with the stigma of a felony or misdemeanor, which excludes them from most well-paying jobs and social acceptance.

There would be an added benefit, which will be discussed in a later chapter. But the drug war is a primary reason behind the instability of the Western Hemisphere. Several Central and Southern American countries have been devastated trying to help the U.S keep drugs out of our neighborhoods. If you really want to see why we have a crisis at our Southern border, look at the impact of our drug policies on foreign communities.

In the 1960s, the American people became aware of a dark and horrific practice in many states of our Union. The publication of *One Flew Over the Cuckoo's Nest,* society was confronted by the state of our mental healthcare system. The conditions were appalling and a documentary by Giraldo Rivera made Americans sick. The inhumane treated of troubled souls drove most to call for change. It was believed that many of those in mental health institutions were persons who could possibly be treated as "out-patients" because their illness was mostly chemical in nature. Many were drug addicts, whose problem was triggered by narcotics use, and therefore helped with methadone treatments.

Movement towards *deinstitutionalization* emptied the cells and did provide freedom for multitudes of victims. But it also abandoned millions to their own devices. The problem was that many states felt that allowing people to be in among the general populations would give them a sense of community and encourage them to continue to help themselves. The reality was that once the mentally ill "felt" better they ceased to continue treatment. It might be just one psychotic episode that led to the loss

Don De Angelo

of a job, money, or housing. Before anyone was aware there was a problem, it was too late! The homeless issue today is in large part a result of this problem.

We are not helping our "general welfare" when we ignore what we can all see with our own eyes. Walk down any city street and those homeless persons on the street are alarmingly unstable. Trying to deal with this as a problem of homelessness and/or poverty is ignoring the real problem.

SHEW Business

What is needed are state and local institutions where persons who are genuinely suffering from mental illness can find the help they need. It is never a positive moment when we must admit that there are simply some people who are incapable of helping themselves.

There will be obvious concerns about a return to potential abuses that have repulsed us. We should understand that we must all exercise extensive vigilance. This primarily means a solid presence of the press. But a federal program is simply not necessary. Mental health, like drug addiction, are best handled in community-like settings. And various states and local realities will vary and should have the flexibility to handle these issues as they see fit. Take these persons off the streets and proper attention can be given to those who are poor because of conditional or situational complications.[50]

When Lyndon Johnson began his War on Poverty the American economy was in a war setting as the president was

---

50   https://journalofethics.ama-assn.org/article/deinstitutionalization-peo ple-mental-illness-causes-and-consequences/2013-10

The American Revolution

preparing to put troops into Vietnam. The level of poverty in the United States in 1965 stood at 19%. Michael Harrington, called the Jacob Riis of the 1960s, wrote of the horrors of a rising class of poor citizens with little access to opportunity. The Democrat administration instituted a barrage of new federal programs to help less-fortunate Americans.

Since 1965, the federal and state governments have spent over $22 trillion on "ending" poverty. The poverty rate today stands at 14%. Any honest assessment would give this project a failed grade. And the real tragedy of all these programs is that poverty in America today is really about subsidy and not remedy. Americans on welfare are not encouraged to change their situation as much as quantify their needs. Meanwhile, we have established at the federal, state, and local levels an enormous bureaucracy costing the taxpayers a fortune. According to a study by the CATO Institute, we are currently spending $1 trillion a year on this collective goal.

Better solution, require every American to make a percentage contribution from their payroll to a welfare charity of their choice. The money would be distributed directly to the charity, eliminating the need for federal and state bureaucracies. The cost goes down and more money goes to help the poor. Ronald Reagan made it a point to demonstrate that nearly 75 cents of every dollar spent on poverty went to government officials. Imagine the amount of help we could provide if we just got rid of the middleman? In 2018, total personal income in the United States was roughly $17.5. trillion[51] If Americans were obligated to divert 5% of their wages to charities of their choice, that

---

51   https://www.statista.com/statistics/216756/us-personal-income/

would be $875 billion going directly to those who help the poor. Make that a real "tithe" and ten percent of all income going to charity would be incredible.

This is not to disparage anyone who works in the federal or state bureaucracy. Most public employees simply want to do a good job and earn[52] a decent living like everyone else. But the idea that we are perpetuating a 19th century administrative order to handle 21st century problems, seems illogical. Virtually every sector of the US economy has had to endure dramatic down-sizing. Over the last 30 years, millions of Americans in the private sector have seen their occupations, let alone their jobs, eliminated. As the government sector takes up more of the U.S. economy, it is both prudent and required that public administration be held to the same standards of efficiency and excellence. If there is simply a better way to fund programs for those most in need, it makes complete sense to streamline these processes regardless of how many government workers are displaced.

It may be that a guaranteed minimal income (GMI) is the better route. States could decide that anyone who has a full-time job should receive a direct payment to raise that salary to a livable one. While it sounds a bit too Marxist for some tastes (certainly mine)– if it can be done with elimination of all other welfare programs, including getting rid of a minimum wage – it may be the best practice given current financial and political realities. The bottom line remains – what we have been doing is too bureaucratic, too complicated, and too expensive and not working. This should only go to citizens of the United States and those

---

52

The American Revolution

with at least 40 hours of work per week, not necessarily at the same job.

The key is we need to shake things up and everyone should be willing to discuss everything to find a better solution. Right now, both parties are getting more attention by virtue signaling their ideological superiority. Voting for third parties will get their attention and force them to sit down and start negotiating.

Immigration Policy

The story line is always the same: We are a nation of immigrants. Go back far enough and everyone is an immigrant. The Asiatic peoples who traversed the Bering Sea and land bridge are the ancestors of our Indian brothers and sisters. The narrative is repeated to promote a specific ideal – all immigration is for the good of the country and the people who choose to come here. Mutually beneficial movement of people seems like a no-brainer. When a company cannot fill a position because there are few if any Americans to apply for the job, the idea that the government would stand in the way of matching the right worker with the job seems counterintuitive.

People who find themselves under unimaginable horrors and threats should always have a friendly and safe place to go. Any society numb to such humanity is unfit to be called civilized. The Pope told us to, "Build bridges, not walls!"

First, let's establish somethings that really should be common knowledge, but have become amazingly controversial. Immigration is not the underlying cause of our nation's woes. There is a net benefit for the United States when a good system is in place.[53] But no nation can exist if it does not have internationally respected borders. A nation is defined in large part on the physical reality of itself: size, geographic descriptions, and borders. Even in an open border construct, the lines between one country and another must be respected by everyone.

The United States will never solve the world's refugee crises. In any given year, there are nearly a billion people in harm's way. Millions of our fellow human beings endure hardships that are sad and unthinkable to us. If we were to double the number of asylum seekers each year, we would still make a tiny dent in the global numbers. The U.S. will NOT solve world poverty by increasing immigration.[54]

There are some very bad people who do genuinely hate this country – what we stand for and the various bad things that were done in our name. These "immigrants" are looking for an easy way into our society so that they might lie-in-wait for an opportunity to inflict terror upon us. The tragedy of 9/11 was as much a result of our collective naivety about the intentions of alien residents as it was about radical Islam. This number is significantly below what many anti-immigration proponents claim, but even a small number of bad people can do considerable damage.

The economic reality of the United States is radically different than at any time in our history. The last major wave of immigration at the turn of the 20th century saw an America with millions of unskilled labor jobs, and plenty of western land to buy if one

---

53   https://www.cato.org/blog/14-most-common-arguments-against-immigra tion-why-theyre-wrong This is a great study of pros and cons.

54   https://www.youtube.com/watch?v=LPjzfGChGlE This is THE best video to watch to get a perspective on the world refugee crisis and our immigration policy.

The American Revolution

preferred farming or ranching. The industrial demands of our economy required a steady flow of new workers willing to put in the long hours at back-breaking tasks. It was a time of no minimum wage or labor standards of any kind.

But those days have long since gone. We are a nation dependent on high-skilled labor and persons without an American high school diploma are typically destined for a life of low income and limited mobility. To bring in more such people will only exacerbate the pressure on this group of citizens already struggling to survive. There is no magic remedy for our own domestic population regarding their economic security, and bringing in more does nothing to help.

There is no quantifiable impact on overall wages from illegal immigration. There is, however, considerable impact on the wages of workers at the lowest rung of earners. When more immigrants come into the country many of the services enjoyed by well-off Americans become cheaper. Because they tend not to be competing with immigrants for jobs, the general impact is positive. If too many immigrants come into the country, there is inevitable downward pressure on wages.

If it is true that immigrants (and specifically illegal immigrants) are not a drain on the health and welfare system, why are so many states rushing to provide such benefits for free? It's a very odd trope to say immigrants are not a burden so let's make them so. All immigrants are a burden initially, but their long-term contribution to American prosperity is why they are celebrated. To openly declare that the government is going to make sure immigrants become an even bigger financial burden seems counterproductive. It merely proves those who harbor anti-immigrant feelings that their worst fears are in fact true.

Don De Angelo

One final fact has to do with the so-called disapproval of our immigrant policy by other countries. It must be understood that no nation in the history of the world has had more immigrants from more parts of the world than the United States. While every immigrant group can claim direct hostility to its introduction to American society, literally millions of foreign-born people have been successfully assimilated into our country. It is the inherent sovereign authority of any nation to determine who enters and/or stays in their country.

The current situation at the Southern border reflects a few historical realities. The United States really didn't have a specific set of rules on immigration until the 1880s. Ellis Island was built not to keep out immigrants but rather to process them in the most orderly way possible. Yes, people were screened for mental illness, criminal records, and communicable diseases. But the real focus was on recording who was coming into the country and where they were planning to settle.

New York City specifically wanted the facility because hordes of people were simply staying where they landed, putting an incredible burden on the local neighborhoods. Everyone has family stories of sneaking into or out of Ellis Island; but the reality is much more benign. The idea of restricting immigration was more a result of the Great Wave of immigration through Ellis Island and the First World War.

The United States first tried to officially restrict immigration in the 1920s. Whether out of fear of Marxist labor unionists infiltrating our industrial work force or a spirit of disillusionment after the Great War; Americans were eager to reembrace the isolationism that many felt was good policy. The quota system implemented permitted a low number of immigrants from

The American Revolution

various ethnic groups, based on their overall numbers reflected in the U.S. Census. It was meant to target primarily Eastern and Southern Europeans, Jews, and Asians. Important to note is that Canadians and Latin Americans were exempt from these laws. There were essentially open borders on both our Northern and Southern flank.

The issue that first impacted our current situation was the Immigration Act of 1965. Here Lyndon Johnson signed a law that ended the quota system and replaced it with overall caps on visa issuances and a first-come-first-serve immigration system. For the first time in American history, Canadians and Latin Americans had to get in line with everyone else to legally enter the United States.

This is not a trivial issue. In fact, since the early 1940s the U.S. and Mexico had entered what were called Bracero Agreements to encourage Mexican men and women to come to work in the United States. Most of these individuals were not coming to be Americans and the migration back-and-forth was a normal part of border life in the Southern United States. All of this changed in 1965.

What we now call the illegal immigration crisis begins here. And, by the 1980s there were signs of discontent everywhere. Ronald Reagan was able to sign a compromise bill in 1986 that was going to end illegal immigration in the country forever. Two elements were at the core of the agreement. First, the United States was going to build a border security apparatus of some kind. Yes, a "wall" was going to be built. Secondly, those persons in the U.S. illegally were to come out of the shadows, admit they were wrong, and then permitted to apply for citizenship – they called it "amnesty."

162

Don De Angelo

The amnesty went forward as planned, the border not so much. Yes, fencing was improved in places. Yes, more Border Patrol officers were hired. Even when multiple budgets included border wall construction, not everything was done. There was certainly more federal bureaucracy created, to process all the new verification documents and background checks. Most importantly, illegal immigration skyrocketed.

If you wonder why there is so much animosity on both sides of this issue, look at the obvious. Democrats see amnesty as a great way to make illegal immigrants feel indebted to them when they vote. Republicans feel that without a wall they are getting no guarantees that illegal immigration won't be perpetual. Because no one wants to give in, and no one trusts the other side to live up to their side of the bargain – nothing happens except rhetoric.

The clearest problem with immigration is that neither main party has proposed any real option for reforming the system. It is wonderful political theater to engage in virtue signaling on this problem. If someone you don't agree with proposes limiting immigration or deporting illegal immigrants – call him a racist. It gets your base voters fired up. But it gets the other side fired up too. When you call someone a racist, they tend not to want to talk to you anymore. To some this serves them well. They continue their rhetoric and can portray themselves as the good guy knowing they will never have to produce a solution.

Since the start of the Biden administration, there has essentially been no border policy. Millions of unvetted people, mostly young men, have flooded the country. Proud *sanctuary* states and cities, entirely Democrat, are suddenly feeling the effects of their generosity. The incompetence of the Department of Homeland Security (DHS) to give the Border Patrol and Customs Offices

The American Revolution

the resources necessary lends credibility to those *conspiracy theorists* who claim it is all designed to destroy our country, steal elections, or both. Even without such claims, the sheer numbers mean extreme pressure on all levels of government.

Try Something New

Any realistic immigration reform law will have to include: (A) A credible border security mechanism; (B) a means by which persons already here are not deported; (C) meaningful criteria for entry into the United States; and (D) a more-friendly environment for those who genuinely want to become a part of the American community. The process is daunting, but we don't even have a working plan to debate. It is time someone put up some blueprint to get a conversation started.

Borders do really matter. It has become a dirty word in some circles, but we really do need to understand that any country that cannot control who enters or leaves it is asking for trouble. Because to the dereliction of Biden administration to control the situation; it will require any new president to order the military to stop the flood of illegal immigrants.

The next step is easier: Ask the Border Patrol agents what they feel they need to tackle the problem. If they say they want a wall – we build a wall. If the men and women who are sworn to protect us say this is what they need then we do it. If we can secure the border with triple fencing instead – great! We certainly need more immigration courts, judges, and public defenders. We may need more money for expanded facilities and proper housing for unaccompanied children who are brought across the border illegally.

Don De Angelo

Once that issue is resolved, there will be a very large consensus to deal humanely with those people coming into our country. It is simply not true that most Americans hate immigrants. We may get impatient when immigrants don't assimilate as fast as we might wish; but most of us love the ideal of our country as a melting pot. But how to make the system better? This proposal involves a **Three-Card** system.

Green Card

The traditional Green Card should only be given to those individuals who are coming the United States because they want to become Americans or they have reasons why they need Permanent Residency. There is a very good argument for increasing the number of these cards being issued. Once obtained, the Immigration and Naturalization Service (INS) should create a predictable and efficient process for Green Card holders to become full citizens. There are millions of people who are ready and able to make great contributions to the United States. The current system discourages those people to even begin a move here. The convoluted process makes illegal entry a logical option and that should never be true. Anyone in the United State with a Green Card who commits a major crime would be placed into a different category.

Yellow Card

Yellow is a warning color. Green Card holders who are in legal trouble or have misbehaved during the naturalization process

The American Revolution

would be moved into this "conditional" status. It would still be possible for the person to recover their Green Card, but they will have to jump through some hoops to prove they are worth the reconsideration.

Yellow Cards would also be issue to any conditional situations of entry. Students, tourist, and workers would fall into this category. Their permission to enter the U.S. has been given under specific conditions and for limited periods of time.

Asylum seekers and refugees would be included in this group. There should be a Congressional ruling that declares which countries have been determined places of crisis, which justifies a person's plea for entrance into the country under such a status. These people should also be considered for a possible Green Card if certain conditions are met.

Currently, the United State makes changing these conditions difficult. If you come here as a student and then want to stay to get a job, you are supposed to leave the country and apply again, unless you have taken the initiative to find a job before your student visa expired and your employer is willing to sponsor you.

There should be a way to "reward" those Yellow Card holders who abide by the stipulations of their visa and want to stay for another purpose that seems rational and reasonable. When someone comes to this country on a student visa and earns their degree – that diploma should come with an automatic Green Card.

Yellow Cards are a middle position. Anyone with a Yellow Card who violates the conditions of their visas would be moved into the final category – Red Cards.

Don De Angelo

Red Cards

A Red Card is the last draw. Anyone with a Red Card is subject to deportation. But a Red Card holder who is not committing additional crimes and is simply in the country illegally would not be sent out of the country.

Whenever anyone comes into the United States illegally, they would be given a Red Card. Possession of this card means that you will *never* become a citizen of the United States, nor be eligible for any federal benefits. You will be permitted to buy property, get insurance on your own, and obtain a driver's license. No one who is deemed not a threat to the United States or its citizens gets deported and no prolonged legal battles.

The new system would allow for faster movement of people through the processing at the border. There seems no reason to hold someone in detention just to prove they are coming from a bad place. Once the person has no criminal record nor harbors terrorist sentiment, they should get their card and move on with their life.

Treat people like adults. Green Cards should be given to people who offer the best possibility of fully assimilating into American political culture. A "merit system" should be established by Congress and reflect the real economic conditions in the United States. But those who come here with pure intentions and show their willingness to be American should not see multiple obstacles in their path.

Foreign and Military Policy

Pax Americana is a term that brings both comfort and fear around the world. The pathway to hegemony is filled with both practical

The American Revolution

progress of events and horrific miscalculations. The history is too much to detail here but the future of America's position as a superpower has a prominent position in our national conversation.

The United States has had a very short history as an interventionist power. While always an aggressive country, Americans have historically preferred to remain out of the affairs of other countries – particularly those outside of the Western Hemisphere.

The major shift in this mindset really occurred after World War II. Prior, the U.S. tried to be both a world power and an isolated nation. This contradictory position created several moments of embarrassing vulnerability. In the war with Spain in 1898, the decision to join World War I, and the attack on Pearl Harbor and mobilization for World War II; made Americans question whether they could continue as a part-time world power. When the USSR began violating the Yalta Conference promises, a terrified Europe turned to the U.S. again and we changed the way we *prepare* for war. Since then, the nation has been in a constant state of war readiness.

When President Eisenhower warned of the perils of a perpetual military-industrial complex (MIC), he was trying to alert his countrymen that a nation always armed for war was more likely to be in one. The contradiction was that Eisenhower's embrace of a policy of containment, meant that the United States was obligated to provide for the military readiness of the entire western alliance. This meant billions of dollars set aside for weapon systems, covert military activities, and never-ending intelligence gathering. None of which is cheap, and it is almost impossible to determine when enough is enough; and weapons manufacturers are more than willing to meet demand.

Don De Angelo

Currently the United States has several hundred military bases all over the world. We sell (and sometimes give away) billions of dollars in weapons and training. Many of my history and government students have no idea that, while technically allies, we still have *occupation* troops in Germany, Italy, and Japan. The Cold War gave strong impetus to sustaining the hyper levels of spending to ensure both we and our allies felt safe in an uncertain world.

It is interesting to study the writings of foreign and military policy personalities immediately following the collapse of the Soviet Union in 1992. Francis Fukuyama wrote that this unique moment meant that the world would never have to be defined or troubled by the global type of conflicts of the past.[55] President George H.W. Bush spoke of a "New World Order" in which the newfound peace would permit the United Nations to function as a true body of international cooperation. It was the impetus for Agenda 30 and the globalist hopes of *one world government* run by elites.

The First Gulf War was in part a demonstration of the power that could be wielded by such a universal alliance. President Bill Clinton took full advantage of this new "peace dividend" and balanced the federal budget for the first time since the 1950s. In fact, had the euphoria continued, Clinton had a projected $2 trillion surplus for the first ten years of the 21st century.

The tragedy of 9/11 changed everything! The hope that Fukuyama was right burned up in the ashes of Ground Zero. Many saw prophetic the writings of one of Fukuyama's mentors,

---

55 Fukuyama, Francis (1989). "The End of History?". *The National Interest* (16): 3–18. ISSN 0884-9382. JSTOR 24027184.

The American Revolution

Samuel P. Huntington. His *Clash of Civilizations and the Remaking of World Order*, seemed to be more realistic to the world we were facing.[56] Was the global order coming together? Or was there an inherent resistance to the very idea of "western civilization"? The implications for American foreign and military policy were monumental.

Americans still held clear memories of the Cold War and the sense of impending threat from an idealistically motivated enemy. The protracted hostility of Islamic extremists looked hauntingly familiar. Part of the congressional analysis of 9/11 was that the U.S. had fallen asleep at the sentry post. Cuts in military spending were blamed for a country unprepared for a surprise attack. Within ten years it was as though the "End of History" was a mere instance in time.

America's military spending skyrocketed as did the numbers of covert actions around the globe. It is said that the first victim of any war is civil liberty, and the "war on terror" has been no exception. Our defense budgets have become sacred to the point that any mention of spending cuts, even fiscal responsibility, leads to accusations of unpatriotic sentiments. The Patriot Act (2001) is a virtual cornucopia of suspended rights, that may never be restored. Even revelations that the federal government was indiscriminately surveilling personal conversations and online communication seems to go on without much public discomfort. The "Twitter Files" scandal currently exposed are a consequence of the surveillance state created by such legislation.

---

56 *Huntington, Samuel P.* (2002) [1997], *The Clash of Civilizations and the Remaking of World Order (The Free Press ed.)*. London: Simon $ Schuster. p. 207f. ISBN 978-0-7432-3149-7.

Don De Angelo

The problem in today's foreign and military policy discourse is that there has been a failure to gain consensus on what exactly should be the overarching vision of our national policy? Are we aiming to be a more powerful if better managed Roman Empire? Could it be that we are hoping to formulate a truly new world order by constructing a "super-NATO" to span the globe? For libertarians, our country should aspire to become the world's largest Switzerland – Armed and ready but openly hostile to no one.

To be quick about it – Switzerland makes its international presence known through its diplomatic and economic prowess. It is no pushover. The Swiss are properly armed and have a clear sense of independent sovereignty. Even Hitler knew not to invade Switzerland. To attain a secure nation, invincible but unthreatening, seems the better angel of our nature.

Thomas Jefferson and Alexander Hamilton had very little in common. In fact, it was a rivalry that created multiple explosive moments in American political history. Both men, however, saw their new nation and an "empire" of republics that would become a global power due to its vast resources and commercial enterprise. While Jefferson and Madison overestimated this power in the early 1800s, later decades would see the United States dominate the second industrial revolution.

Does the world need American power? Certainly. Does the United States offer a better option as a peace-enforcement power instead of say Russia or China? Hopefully. The question that still needs to be asked: Does the United States have to continue to be a world power in the manner to which it became known? To this one could argue, in no way whatsoever. We have an opportunity to assert our power in a way more aligned with our ideals and to push the world into a new narrative.

The American Revolution

The Middle East

No region of the world creates more anxiety and frustration for Americans than the Middle East. Few of us understands the complexities of Arab, Muslim, Jewish, and Christian rivalries, and the dynamics of the region's balance of power. Outside of the known terrorist threats, most Americans would just prefer to leave the entire area alone. Should we? Can we?

The solution must be comprehensive but certain things should be appreciated. The United States will never solve the Middle East's religious and political chaos and violence. The best we can aspire to is to provide a "safe" environment for the region to negotiate their issues. Unfortunately, the U.S. has a long history of intervention so disengagement will be significantly difficult. The first step will be to publicly acknowledge our tinkering in the region created many of the problems and we are prepared to change course. It seems most likely that we must now rely on other powers to step in to play the role of diplomacy – Switzerland, Norway, Canada, or Australia. These are all nations not associated with imperial designs or military interventions. And it is OK. Why should we care how a problem gets resolved if it is resolved?

The center of the problem is Israel's existence. And the real fundamental truth is the moment that Palestine is an independent nation, it will seek ways to attack Israel in the hope of wiping it off the planet. The mini-Holocaust of October 7, 2023, should settle any notion that the *two-state solution* has any chance of success at this point. There can be no doubt that, were the Arab nations that surround and constantly threaten Israel were to suddenly stop their aggression and make a peace treaty with Israel,

Don De Angelo

there would be peace in the Middle East. There should also be no illusions that Iran poses the largest threat to this peace.[57]

It is a true shame that the narrative on the region has never included an honest grasp of these truths. Rather than find a suitable place for the Arabs in Palestine to live and work, there has been instead a decision to use the sufferings of these people as a bludgeon to continually attack Israel. This is not to say that the Israeli's have been completely innocent victims of Arab hostility. But the fact that the last 70 years have been used to exploit the suffering of millions of people has squandered billions of dollars that could have instead been used to establish new homes and lives for these beautiful people.

And the West must come to terms with its own role. The Jews were persecuted in the West. The Holocaust was not just a German atrocity – it was a catastrophe of Western Civilization. To atone for such a horrific treatment, the collective reparation was the recreation of Israel and the establishment of self-determination of the Jewish people. The Israeli people swore, "Never Again!" and they mean it. For us all to stand around today and pretend that we didn't understand what that meant is disingenuous, at the very least. That Israel is the only nation that seems to get its hands tied when it defends itself is testament to the continuing anti-Semitism of the United Nations and the Arab world.

It is also unfortunate that the common threat by Iran has only recently given impetus to greater cooperation between Arabs and

---

57   https://www.jstor.org/stable/10.2979/israelstudies.23.3.28?seq=1#page_ scan_tab_contents If there is to be peace between Arabs and Jews there needs to be a new formula.

The American Revolution

Israelis. President Biden's inconsistent and feeble foreign policy has ruined that cooperation and we see Iran and Saudi Arabia in a new reproachment. U.S. foreign policy should have been and should now be to encourage such a reality and to step aside for other diplomatic efforts by nations such as Norway and/or Switzerland. Someday, when America becomes less of a threat, we might be able to be the broker of peace; but given our recent record of intervention and destabilization, it is impossible to pretend we are an "honest" broker.

The most important element to our role in the Middle East is our own energy policy. While energy policy is covered in a later chapter on the environment; dependence on the region's oil and gas makes us vulnerable to the instability there. To ease that pressure American oil and natural gas production should be increased to give alternative sources of energy to our European and Asian allies. The United States, Canada, and Mexico could unleash their reserves and bring economic relief to millions and help remove a major reason why we remain entangled in this region. This would give the U.S. breathing room to allow for more introspective analysis and less pressure to "solve" strategic problems.

Russian and NATO

It seemed that NATO was most likely a dinosaur in a post-Cold War world. The U.S./Russian relationship of the 1990s never foreshadowed the level of tension that would emerge under Vladimir Putin. The United States is partly to blame because we perceived Russia as a fallen enemy worthy of pity and

Don De Angelo

patronization. When the crises began in the former Yugoslavia, Russia found itself kept outside the international conversation. While there may have been, little Russia could have done in real terms, its historical role as the "defender of the Slavic people" caused a sense of resentment among the Russian people. This was particularly true when President Clinton supported the creation of Kosovo at the expense of Serbia, a long-time ally of Russia. The expansion of NATO further and further into the Russian "comfort zone of defense" was not a sign of security for Russia but rather a sign of aggression by western powers.

Putin exploited such slights as his rationale for Russia's return to a more autocratic society. When he lamented the collapse of the Soviet Union as the greatest disaster of the 20th century, he was laying out his vision of territorial designs in Eastern Europe. There is little evidence that it meant possessing territory, but an expectation that the governments on Russia's western frontier were not openly hostile. The basic demand is that NATO cannot be in a geopolitical advantage. He was able to equate the economic chaos and suffering of the 1990s to shrinking Russian world power status. He coopted both nationalists and former communists into a coalition of reactionary populism. If the people of Russia would give him autocratic power to reassert Russian imperial designs, it will result in an increase in Russian prosperity and security. His invasion of Ukraine and seizure of Crimea should have surprised no one. And so far, he is getting amazing leverage with his people.

Unfortunately, this has ended any conversations about ending the NATO alliance. Regardless of the harsh rhetoric of President Donald Trump, now is not the time to abandon our friends under threat of Russian aggression. The Baltic states, Poland, Romania,

The American Revolution

and Bulgaria must know that our commitment to their security and sovereignty is unwavering. But we must do this in a pragmatic and realistic manner. Realist foreign policy is needed. Ukraine cannot defeat Russia regardless of how much military hardware and intelligence we give. The idea that we could use the Ukrainians to weaken Russia was not only foolish but cruel. There is no courage or valor in a willingness to fight *our* enemy down to the last Ukrainian. Russia has expressed what it needs to start talking. It is time to sit down at the table and end the conflict.

President Trump is correct about one thing. The Europeans have been taking advantage of American largess for far too long. When a Bernie Sanders talks euphorically about the generous welfare states of Scandinavia, he forgets to mention that much of that generosity was based on the underwriting of most of their defense spending. This meant they could reserve more resources for their own population's comfort – less guns, more butter. The NATO leaders know full well they are in arears with the U.S. Germany alone could easily handle their internal defense infrastructure but instead allow the Americans to maintain vast bases on their sovereign territory and continue to cannibalize their own military establishment. There is very little rational excuse for our continued "occupation" of Germany. The only good thing from the war in Ukraine is the final resolve of our NATO partners to foot more of the bill. If this conflict can be brought to a peaceful end, it should be done as quickly as possible. When it does end the U.S. should immediately negotiate an end to NATO as a standing military presence.

The United States should operate with one central truth about our perceived "enemy" – Russia is a dying power. While

Don De Angelo

Mr. Putin has been able to exploit the anxiety of the Russian people to expand his own personal power, he has not even begun to plan for the reality of Russian governance when he eventually leaves power. The Russian population continues to deteriorate as fewer and fewer choose to procreate. In fifty years, the Russian hinterland could become virtually unpopulated.

Putin's additional error is that he is chumming up with fellow *thugacracy* China in the disillusion that they are natural allies. But China has the patience of a tiger. Siding with a dying Russia allows China to preoccupy America in Europe so it can continue to harass its Asian neighbors, especially Taiwan. Eventually, when the U.S. is preoccupied and Russia is on its literal knees, China will complete its hegemonic designs in Asia and try gobble up eastern regions of present-day Russia. The enemy of my enemy is my friend, until they no longer needed, then my weakened *friend* becomes my prey. This truth should offer a pathway to negotiation.

The U.S. should make its commitment to NATO based on its help to Eastern Europe and insist that Western Europe take up the slack regarding their own defense. If a miracle could happen and Russia wakes up from their self-inflicted daydream a truly peaceful Europe is entirely possible, and America should immediately seek a departure from day-to-day presence on the continent. Europe can heal Europe only if it wants to. The United States tried to play a "winning strategy" of keeping Europe afraid of Russia. There was no virtue in isolating Russia simply because Putin is not a nice man. Foreign policy is filled with strange bed fellows. Putin wanted integration into the European order and was rejected because the U.S. saw itself in the 1990s as the singular hegemon and thought keeping Russia on its knees was

The American Revolution

in our national interest. The *unipolar* hegemony was an arrogant and selfish mistake that has reaped the whirlwind.

China

There can be no doubt that China poses the greater threat, in the long term. This is something of a self-inflicted reality as we, and most of the world, rushed to embrace China as it emerged from its hermit status to seek capitalist solutions to its abject poverty. In the desire to sell to a billion people, the West quickly abandoned its practical skepticism and created an easy path for China to enter the World Trade Organization (WTO). The rapid economic growth of China is directly responsible for China's growing military prowess. Without access to international markets, there would be no Chinese blue navy nor financial underwriting of North Korea. Our corporate elite sold us out for big profits, although they also gave away many of their technological advantages.

But the die has been cast. China is a world power and could become a very dangerous enemy to freedom and stability. But again, this does not justify a reinforcement of perpetual warmongering on the part of the United States. Japan and South Korea, along with other regional powers, have an intense incentive to vigilance. We must support them but remember that our economic reality will limit our ability to threaten large scale military vengeance. China still has major internal problems. Ethnic animosity is a constant threat to the communist party's hold on power. There is also a massively disproportional economic development going on in China. This uneven growth causes discontent that is not easily controlled. There is an unspoken dilemma of population collapse. It may seem counter-logical to discuss such an issue regarding China, but its one-child policy may have permanently damaged its ability to sustain long-term economic security with a rapidly aging workforce.

And ultimately, China is in a sort of *Gilded Age* in which it is seeing incredible economic growth and expansive external power. But it has massive internal insecurity and eventually will have to deal with these inconsistencies. Policies on population control are already proving devastating to the country. There will be a moment when the Chinese people will insist on a level of personal freedom to match their economic security, a degree of status and agency until now unheard of. The United States should use this fact to keep from becoming paranoid about short-term, perceived threats and mimic China's ability to be patient and wait for more favorable circumstances. If China wants to invest in its recreation of the silk road trading infrastructure on its own dime – let them. We will soon realize that to act in haste or panic is to play directly into the Chinese designs. China wants us to make easy mistakes that can be exploited for perceived big gains in territorial largess or superiority. Americans have not been historically known as a patient world power – time to grow up.

Military Budgets

Something that must be understood about budgetary issues involving the military is that defense is an expressed power of the federal government. This means that only the federal government has the power to manage our nation's defenses. When politicians

The American Revolution

act nonchalant about our national security by engaging in jingoisms, it is irresponsible and dangerous. But does that mean that the military budget should be treated as a sacred obligation?

When the end of the Cold War was seen as a moment for budgetary review, the Congress began literally shutting down bases all over the United States and the world. This process provided many states and localities with massive property for economic projects. Some took these bases for government purposes (such as colleges in California). The loss of such long-term obligations made a huge difference in defense budgets.

The armed forces also began to privatize many jobs usually done by recruits. Contractors now vie for lucrative projects doing even mundane things such as laundry and food provisions or even janitorial services. The key savings came in not having to finance the long-term obligations that came with using uniformed employees. Just the G.I. Bill benefits amounted to millions of dollars and pension savings could reach billions.

The current dilemma is that everyone is looking for that kind of savings today. The United States certainly doesn't have to be married to the idea of being the world's police force; but there remain major threats to our security, and we need to remain vigilant to expanding and newer challenges. So, where is the savings? Does the U.S. need all branches of the armed services to be of equal levels of readiness?

Lacking all the information and education about military expenditures and strategy priorities, makes definitive proposals impossible. The repeated stories of billions in unaccounted purchases and lost material sent to allies, makes every taxpayer angry. It should not, therefore, prevent us from having conversations about alternatives.

Don De Angelo

It seems that our navy should be the focus of our international readiness. China's most direct threat to us and our Asia/Pacific allies is the creation of a deep-sea navy. While the current level of build-up is nowhere near our own present dominance, this cannot be taken for granted. The goal of China is to rival our dominance and they seem determined to accomplish this as quickly as possible.

Our navy must keep pace and always maintain superiority. This is the best protection against Chinese encroachment on our territorial waters and give our allies a sense of security, which will help to keep tensions low. Global reach will be necessary but may not require all the current bases being maintained by the United States. Could the British, French, and other Europeans be capable of keeping vigil with their own carrier groups? Then, more saving can be found, but never at the expense of vigilance. We should only be where other allies cannot patrol.

In addition, the US Air Force is paramount to our national security and the need to be a presence globally at any given moment. This will also require a massive financial commitment. It is unavoidable if we are to establish the international understanding that we are to be left alone. Only when this perception is permanent can we begin to reestablish ourselves as primarily a commercial and economic power in the manner of Switzerland. "Peace through strength" should never be a cliché.

The remaining branches should be viewed with more flexibility. It could mean that the army could be based more on state national guard forces and reserves. Again, this is not a definitive proposal but a point of conversation. We should be open to inventive variations and not tied to traditional territorial grievances between the branches or emotional memories of past

The American Revolution

glories. Literally dozens, if not hundreds of foreign bases should be closed. American secret operations in Africa, Asia, and Latin America should be ended. The weight of security should be for us alone. The notion that military interventions in obscure places overseas is directly linked to our national security has been destroyed by recent adventures in Afghanistan, Iraq, Syria, Libya, and now Ukraine.

War Powers Amendment

No greater respect can be afforded our brave men and women than to extremely limit their use. The fact is America is too quick to go to war. We are engaged in places that have no real barring on national security and provide reasons for foreign resentment and future incidents of blowback. Again, the problem is the U.S. Constitution has a structural check-and-balance that allows for behavior that can only be seen as passing-the-buck. The president is the Commander-in-Chief of armed forces, but the Congress has power of the purse and the power to formally declare war.

Since World War II, the national government has been unwilling to follow their respective responsibilities under the constitution. All our military escapades since 1941 have been through various forms of authorizations to use force. Using resolutions allows any congress to obfuscate its own commitment. Giving the executive the authority to decide when and how to use our armed forces allows representatives and senators to have it both ways. Should the exercises prove successful, they can take credit for having given the authorization. Conveniently the opposite

Don De Angelo

also proves effective. If the "president's war" proves a failure or lack public support, these same legislators can insist that they had no responsibility. Witness Hillary Clinton's tortured logic to explain her support for the *Authorization to Use Force* in Iraq as a vote for military support without condoning President George W. Bush's decision to use force!

The U.S. Constitution must be amended to clarify the responsibility of each of our government's branches. We have a model in the War Powers Act, which was enacted during the Vietnam War era. Presidents should have the authority to use all military assets to repel an attack directly on America or its citizens. Should a U.S. military asset be attacked, no president should feel restrained by an obligation to report immediately to congress and request permission to act.

Such power should not be interpreted as a blank check. Such a situation occurred in 1964, when an invented attack on U.S. forces in the Gulf of Tonkin, was used by President Johnson to expand our presence in Vietnam. The War Powers Act calls on presidents to gain congressional approval for any continued military action beyond 90 days. This seems reasonable and should be a mandatory and permanent part of our national security decision-making.

Additionally, it seems prudent to require that any further military activity against a foreign enemy must require a formal declaration of war by the U.S. Congress and set into motion certain wartime conditions. First there should be an activation of the selective service laws. Individuals of draft age should be notified of their potential responsibility to report for active duty. Next, Congress must identify all necessary financial means of supporting the designated war objectives. This should include

The American Revolution

taxes on wealthy Americans who will be the least likely to be called upon to make the ultimate sacrifice and may if fact financially profit from a wartime economy. War is a dire reality that should be treated as such. Our current behavior allows all of us to go on with our lives as though nothing is happening. Meanwhile, thousands of our finest citizens are literally fighting for their lives.

In peacetime, the military budget should only increase by the rate of annual inflation. Everything about the military budget should be scrutinized for the fraud and gauging that seems endemic of military contracting. Those who serve in the defense department should never be allowed to go into lobbying for military contractors and no members of the military-industrial-complex should run the Pentagon. No one should profit from the serious reality of war. Requiring a serious approach to engaging in war will hopefully limit it becoming the first option of American foreign policy.

Jaw Jaw, not War War

American diplomacy has suffered a great deal since the horrors of 9/11. For the United States to evolve into a more secure power without the paranoia that seems more appropriate for Russia or China, we need to invest in our foreign services. This will require major expansion of diplomatic activity and training. We need our most talented people to commit to careers serving our nation in this capacity. This is much cheaper that long-term wars of choice and nation-building operations. It will also begin to restore America's reputation as one favoring dialogue and cultural

Don De Angelo

exchange. The current story of the United States and its allies actively trying to prevent peace negotiations in Ukraine is indefensible. There is zero virtue in bravely fighting the Russians to the last Ukrainian.

Again, it is important to understand that only the federal government has the power to engage in such activity. While several federal departments could and should be eliminated, this is an area where there must be a resolute commitment to excellence. The time has come to break up the Central Intelligence Agency (CIA). There may be several potential terror attacks that might have been stopped, but at the expense of our precious civil liberties. The State Department (or what would be the Department of Foreign Affairs) should do most of our intelligence gathering.

Additionally, it is a good idea for the American people to commit more support for assistance to developing nations through free trade and better access to American markets. Giving away food and money seems like a nice thing to do, but growing economies based on market forces is the only way to create vibrant, and therefore stable, nations. The United States could set the example by creating a free trade agreement with Latin America.

Environmental Policy

The new religion of many political activists has become the environmental movement. The word religion is applicable because some have become zealous in their demands for government action regarding climate change and the drive to a carbon-free world. It also a movement based more on feelings and beliefs than true scientific observation. Read Michael Shellenberger's,

The American Revolution

Apocalypse Never and you will get the difference. The euphoria from a sense of making a real difference can push people into behavior that eliminates any chance of compromise, because it is seen as a failure to defeat a perceived enemy. It is no different than the hysteria after 9/11 and the war on terror.

There is little use in delving into the science of climate change or the arguments of whether any one side is right or wrong. It is sufficient to state that a cleaner environment, regardless of the motivation, is a good thing. This reality does not excuse bad policy or wasteful spending. A desire to remove millions of cars from highways is not a rationale for building a $77 billion high-speed train that few people will ever use in California, for example.[58]

One important reality that the religious environmentalists refuse to acknowledge is that solar and wind power will never meet the energy demands of modern society. Neither of these sources of energy are sufficient to meet expanding electricity use. For logistical and structural reasons this will never work.[59]

In addition, both sources of energy come with very non-eco-friendly consequences. To make solar farms viable there must be massive destruction of desert eco-systems. The desert landscapes are most often permanently damage and multiple endangered species harmed. Wind farms are killing hundreds if not thousands of birds, mostly the most endangered birds of prey. Is it the price we are supposed to pay for a carbon-free economy?

---

58 https://reason.org/commentary/california-overstates-bullet-trains-climate-benefits/ This boondoggle would be hysterical if it weren't such a financial disaster for the state.

59 https://www.youtube.com/watch?v=N-yALPEpV4w Michael Shellenberger is a great person to listen to as he was/is a big environmentalist who speaks from first-hand experience.

Don De Angelo

This is what causes so much cynicism among anti-environmentalists who already may doubt the *science* behind the climate change agenda. The inability to accept an error in implementation causes an entire enterprise to be challenged. The costs rise and increasing taxpayer subsidies makes the position of environmentalists even more uncertain. Renewable energy is not cost effective. It requires massive subsidization by federal, state, and even local governments.

Even electric cars are nefarious in their existence. If one examines the amount of energy it takes to build each "green" car, it is never really ameliorated by its operation. Many of the rare earths used in their manufacture come from some of the most oppressive regimes in the world. The mining of these minerals is done in places with none of the environmental safeguards that would be exercised in an American operation. It is easy to be smug about one's own environmental superiority when the real environmental impact on one's rhetoric is not immediately visible to one's own community. If America wants these technologies, then it should only use domestically sourced raw materials. If damage is to be done to landscapes to feed our energy needs, then we should bear it here.

If clean energy is the true goal, then there are limited options. The best market-based assessment is to turn to nuclear energy using thorium. This element is more abundant and less volatile than uranium and has a dramatically lower half-life. It requires a much smaller footprint and can burn more efficiently. Allowing the free market to construct and operate these energy plants could make the U.S. electricity generation completely carbon-free within 20 years. Just approve one blueprint for a small, medium, and large facility and then get the government

The American Revolution

out of the way. But the same people demanding cleaner energy are also committed to an ending nuclear anything. Their inability to be open to thorium demonstrates their religious-like, narrow-mindedness.[60]

While always needful of caution and safety, we must be more willing to explore this and other options. It is un-libertarian to insist that fellow citizens in West Virginia turn to nuclear energy if coal is a cheaper option. Does the goal of a true green world mean everything? Then we will have to destroy every hydroelectric plant. They destroy rivers and entire valley ecosystems. Solar farms destroy vast areas of desert landscapes and lose vast amounts of energy during transmission. Wind farms are responsible for the deaths of thousands of large, predatory birds, many endangered. In our delusional quest to "save the planet" we are destroying the environment.

Again, it is the belief of most libertarians that states, and local communities should be free to decide what works best for them. Some options like thorium may provide the answer. But having the federal government impose one solution on everyone is neither democratic nor a formula for success. Federal subsidies for "green" options that we know are not self-sustaining is not only irresponsible but immoral, given what those same dollars could be used for.

From 2001 to 2013 I owned a home in San Diego, California. My roof had a 180-degree, southern exposure. This meant that I could have installed solar panels, which would have provided all the energy necessary. The Obama administration and the state of

---

60 https://www.youtube.com/watch?v=tHO1ebNxhVI Watch this TED talk and get educated about safer and more efficient nuclear power.

Don De Angelo

California both offered taxpayer funded subsidies for me to install the solar panels. But because it was a government program, so there were strings attached.

First, I could not go off the grid. Even though my panels could store up enough energy for me to survive alone, I was required to sell my energy to the grid. Not only that, but I would have to pay the utility company for the use of their wires to sell that power. Then, when I ran out of power, I would buy energy from the utility.

Second, the law(s) were written to help domestic manufacturers of solar panels and installation equipment. This meant that the costs for installing the system was going to be higher than market prices. So, a system that should have cost me maybe $12,000 was easily $23,000, before buying battery storage.

Third, the pressure was on to finance the system. This now meant that I would pay above market prices and pay finance charges for a system that still would mean me buying some of my electric from the utility company. Up to 20 years of financing is ridiculous when you consider that the solar panels have only a 20-year lifespan, which means perpetual debt for cleaner energy.

Fourth, no one yet knows how we are going to dispose of these solar panels in a way that is ecofriendly. The panels have toxic materials and cannot simply be tossed in the garbage. This is also true of wind turbines. We are not even sure if anything can be recycled. This is a policy that was simply not well thought out and has minimal positive effect on lowering carbon emissions. The policy ideations begin to look childish in that a committee decides they can save the planet with some pie-in-the-sky program. There is dreamed up financing scheme that usually promises unrealized revenue and then everyone goes full speed ahead.

The American Revolution

Even when the policy exposes the evident miscalculations and unrealistic outcomes, the policy makers double down and refuse to admit defeat. Only the corporate and government elites, who had insider information about green policies, made out well. In fact, most have become millionaires.

What should be the first question asked of everyone is: "What am I prepared to go without in order to save energy?" To insist that others make sacrifices before you take steps to lower your own "footprint" is un-American and illogical. Let the wealthy buy all the solar panels they want and go completely off the grid. They can afford the costs without government subsidies and the burden of disposal. That would take pressure off the grid and allow for more green energy like thorium to be used.

If you drive a Tesla or Chevy Volt you are engaged in a form of virtue signaling. The only reason many of you could afford an electric car is due to subsidies paid to manufacturers and your tax breaks financed by all taxpayers, regardless of their income. We have taken money from people who couldn't afford an EV even with the government-funded reductions for wealthy people to demonstrate how superior they are in reducing their carbon footprint, which has an minuscule impact on global warming at all. And this is being done when we have over one trillion dollars in deficits every year.[61]

The government will never solve the nation's energy problems, let alone end climate change --- only the market can do that. Thorium nuclear energy is already proven and could be in place by market forces within a decade. Companies moving many administrative tasks online has provided fewer commuting hours,

---

61   https://www.youtube.com/watch?v=17xh_VRrnMU The Real Cost!

Don De Angelo

which will truly lessen carbon footprints. The U.S. Department of Energy is a wasteful agency based on these useless practices and would be better off closed.

If the climate change disaster predicted by its promoters is truly this awful, government monies would be better spent in adapting infrastructure to accommodate the rising sea levels and longer droughts. The planet has changed its climate for billions of years and species have come and gone because of an inability to adapt. If the coming apocalypse is as close as believed by the elites who are profiting by its prediction; then let's focus our collective attention on how we survive. Standing at the water's edge trying to turn back the tide is either naïve or arrogant – neither solves the problem and we all just look ridiculous!

Other Expendables

The idea that the federal government must be the first and last resort for our collective happiness is a very sad situation. We have become addicted to various parts of federal spending. It would be hypocritical of me to not admit that my own career has been dependent on government spending. My second master's degree was funded in part by Congressional support of the James Madison Memorial Fellowship Foundation. This reality does not diminish the need to fix the system.

There is no question that it is fun to think of all the cool things we could get from a generous government budget. But should we keep on using the credit card for temporary comforts when we know that not a single civilization in history has been able to spend its way into longevity, let alone prosperity?

The American Revolution

The Third Rail

This is the Achilles heel of every attempt at getting a balanced budget in America. There are many misconceptions about the program to begin with; but the powers supporting it are so very strong that any politician who dares touch it risks a dead career.

First, there is no such thing as a "Social Security Trust Fund." This myth was started in the 1980s when smaller populations of older Americans realized short-term surpluses in social security revenues. The practice continued into the 1990s, and part of the wonderful budget surpluses of the Clinton administration included IOUs placed in the Social Security accounts.

The famous "Lock Box" for such funds was coined by then Vice-President Al Gore in the 2000 debates with George W. Bush. The idea was that the government takes your contributions and sets up an account of sorts with your name on it. You pay into the system while you work and when you retire there is a pot of money waiting. This is simply not true.

Social Security is a pay-as-you-go system. The current workers are taxed, and that money is used to pay for the current retirees. The amount each person receives is based on a calculation of the contributions made and the number of years the individual made the contributions. These data are mixed into an actuarial accounting formula that assigns a benefit. The fact that any American who paid into the system must get a payout is what it is considered an *entitlement*. What most Americans do not realize is that there is no constitutional mandate to provide such a benefit. There is however a constitutional mandate to pay our debts, even if it is only to pay the interest. If push ever comes to shove, retirees will be the ones cut off, not our creditors.

Don De Angelo

The program was started during the Great Depression. Many older Americans had done what they believed was the right thing. They put some of their earnings into savings so that when they were older there would be a "nest egg" of money to sustain them. But, with the collapse of hundreds of banks in the 1930s, many of these elderly people had their entire life's savings wiped out. Some became indigents dependent on their children or charity. Those who were still working were forced to stay on the job.

Social Security was meant to do two primary things. First, it was meant to give each worker over 65 a monthly stipend to pay bills. For a retired person or couple, the $200 monthly payment was enough to keep their home, which was usually paid off, and get staples for their personal needs. It was meant to be completely spent each month.

Secondly, the government hoped that a guaranteed monthly payment would incentivize older workers to give up their jobs and retire. This in theory would allow employers to hire younger workers who were unable to find jobs. Most employers did not do this but instead saved the money from lower headcount.

The intent was that when savings were restored to normal levels, and the job market stabilized, the federal program would cease. But most economists knew that the Second World War had spurred the GDP upwards and not the New Deal. When the war appeared to be ending, many feared that another recession or worse was going to happen.

It was Harry Truman who decided to make Social Security a permanent benefit but did not change the formula for its financing. The Baby Boomers were a boon to the system because they so vastly outnumbered their elders. When they became the main

The American Revolution

income earners, the amount of money going into Social Security (and Medicare) was more than what was needed in payments.

But rather than using those monies to establish a true "trust fund" that earned good returns and created additional wealth for the system; the money was used to either finance debts through purchasing bonds or using the money to offset other budget items. Now that the Baby Boomers are retiring in greater numbers every year, their demand on benefits will outpace collections of contributions from current workers. The burden on future earners is even greater than what we are experiencing now.

Any attempt to even discuss fixing this system has become a dangerous prospect. The American Association for Retired Persons (AARP) is the nation's most powerful interest group. It has over 39 million members and earned over $1 billion in 2008. This group will use that pot of money to go after anyone who proposes changing our retirement system.[62] And yet, 24 percent of the 2017 budget went to social security payments.[63]

To suggest that there can never be a change to a system that now has a long-term deficit projection of some $43 TRILLION seems irresponsible.[64] The proposal from the Democratic party is currently to raise the tax rates on higher earners and Republicans are calling for lower inflation-indexing to save money. The idea

---

62   https://humanevents.com/2010/03/25/wealthy-aarp-one-countrys-most-powerful-lobbies/?utm_referrer=https%3A%2F%2Fwww.google.com%2F

63   https://www.cbpp.org/research/federal-budget/policy-basics-where-do-our-federal-tax-dollars-go

64   https://thehill.com/opinion/finance/443465-social-security-just-ran-a-9-trillion-deficit-and-nobody-noticed

Don De Angelo

to "privatize" the fund has been portrayed by the Left as "running grandma off the cliff."[65]

As a younger generation of Americans come into their adult lives, Baby Boomers would do them a great service by supporting a move away from this government-sanctioned Ponzi scheme. But what might it look like. The framework would have to include both fairness and financial viability.

Perhaps we could start by agreeing that every American was going to be responsible for a 10% contribution to their retirement. No matter what point in the working life you are at, you would be making this commitment. This would be the foundation of the fairness situation. No one could complain that they are making a bigger sacrifice.

For those 50 years of age or older, the current system must be kept in place. To make a drastic elimination of social security benefits would be inexcusable and would never pass in any Congress. But those individuals would have to increase their FICA tax rate to 10%. And, it might have to be on all income without expanded benefits. The key is that these individuals would be guaranteed their full benefits under current actuarial calculations.

People from 30-49 would perhaps have 5% of their money continue going into social security in exchange of half of the current projected benefits. The other 5% would be contributed to a private retirement fund (IRA, 401K, 403B). This transitional group would have enough time to adjust and have a partial "safety net" to avoid significant hardships.

---

65   *https://www.youtube.com/watch?v=OGnE83A1Z4U*

The American Revolution

Those currently under 30 would be moved to private investments that are currently used and should remain restricted by law. The government does not give better returns over the lifetime of a worker, so people should be encouraged to have a ten percent savings rate.

Who knows if this is the answer, but it is a model and a starting point for discussion. The truth however is that doing nothing or simply raising the existing taxes is not a formula for success, nor will it improve the retirement security of younger Americans. It will only guarantee future fiscal and monetary problems.

Department of Education

The problems with education are not national. They are local and personal. The drive to reform education has siphoned money away from communities into a vast abyss of educational bureaucracy that has done nothing to effect better teaching in the classroom. The only accomplishment of centralized curriculum reformers was to openly imbed cultural Marxism into our K-12 education systems. It would take another entire book to list out the problems or discuss the best remedies possible. The variables are too complicated and depend on knowledge of unique scenarios based on local realities.

The federal Department of Education has a minimal impact on state and local school spending but requires a mountain of administrative oversite to receive those funds. Many states spend more on complying with federal mandates than they receive in actual cash. It's a lose-lose situation.

Don De Angelo

Here we see more virtue signaling. Federal lawmakers want to be seen as "helping" improve education. Teachers' Unions want to appear to be getting the resources needed to make schools successful. Vote for more money, create a new agency, and say you did your part. But you really didn't change anything except to remove the local community from the conversation, and burden teachers with mandated curriculum.

Shut down the Department of Education and insist that states and local communities do whatever they feel needs to be done to fix the problems. The constitution never intended the federal government to run schools and most Framers were weary of a nationally proscribed educational system. COVID school lockdowns gave most American parents their first real look into *what* was being taught. Instead of teaching children *how* to think they are indoctrinating students on what to think. The outrage should tell us that a top-down curriculum is never acceptable. When it is evident that there is more indoctrination than education happening, and the outrage turns to calls for a mass exodus. Get rid of this bureaucracy and save billions of dollars.

The money given to colleges and universities through direct government aid and subsidized loans need to stop. The taxpayers, most of whom never go to college, should not be coerced to finance institutions that have such open hostilities to Western culture and American values. Many of these elite institutions have large endowments that could easily finance scholarships. Without the free-flowing government dollars, schools will be forced to end their inflationary tuition policies.

The American Revolution

"Endowments"

There is no such thing as a federal endowment. These are euphemisms to lure American taxpayers into willingly giving up more of their hard-earned money. If there were an endowment for the arts, then after a certain number of years-worth of contributions, there would be an enormous investment fund that would allow the institution to function without any additional contributions.

Whether we are talking about arts, humanities, or sciences, the federal contributions were operating funds not sustaining investments. This means that these very noble organizations are perpetually dependent on the government largess. We end up with very politically charged environments where there never should be any such involvement.

Make a sizable, one-time contribution to these institutes that are deemed sufficient for their long-term sustainability and let them loose. If they cannot manage these funds properly and go out of business, then so be it. It may be necessary to insist on board positions for members of Congress to ensure these monies are not squandered. Get the government out of areas of subjective learning and expression. Have universities bid to incorporate these institutions onto their campuses.

Agriculture

No one seems to touch this subject because it effects too man electoral votes. Not that anyone singular state would be critical; but there are so many states dependent on agribusiness, the aggregate

198

impact is substantial. Nevertheless, the amount of money set aside for subsidies and research is not logical. Government payments for farmers not to grow is also ridiculous considering the number of persons who supposedly go hungry every day.

Think about this reality. We currently subsidize multiple products to ensure that the price of commodities stay artificially high. This, along with tariffs on imported agriculture, creates an artificially expensive food market for consumers. Low-income people are therefore at risk of being undernourished and therefore require assistance. We therefore pay for food stamps and other welfare programs to ensure that most Americans can eat. No one has been able to really give a logical explanation as to why this makes sense.

Now, if the American farmer is truly the best – and it certainly seems true from the outside looking in – why do they need government intervention? Is it because other countries do the same for their growers? Then those governments are on the path to fiscal insanity.

The system we now have creates an artificial market, which can encourage some farmers to take additional risks that would not be warranted in a normal economic evaluation. Commodities are the most volatile investments. Making plans based on produce sales is extremely risky. Anything that skews the market can lead many to become overleveraged and eventually bankrupt. There must be a better way.

It may become necessary to begin the reforms with a major payout to get farmers out of debt. The goal however should be to eliminate government intervention in the price of commodities. Food should be as cheap as possible so that the poorest among us can obtain their sustenance with minimal expense.

The American Revolution

No free trade agreement should happen without a mutual commitment to end such practices. The Northern countries should feel good about accepting produce from Southern nations during the winter and vice versa. The aim should be to get the highest quality food at the lowest possible price. Year-round access to fresh produce is a nutritional boon for everyone.

There could be a way to help farmers with short-term lending that seems to be missing from the established banking system. The Populists called for a sub-treasury system back in the late 19th century. While it would be best to allow the private sector to devise short-term lending at below market rates, this banking idea would have allowed the post office to use federal money to lend to farmers at below market rates, purely for seasonal purposes. This would not only ease pressures on farmers but could give the US Postal Service an actual function that would be profitable. They could do the same for "payday loan" customers. Libertarians would privatize all of it.

Corporate Welfare

Here is where we see the double standard of the business world. They object to any interference of the government, until they want a handout from the government. Business lobbyists are the first to complain when a new regulation or tax is introduced that will impact their bottom line. But these same "small government" types will be the first to have their hands out if the think they can get "free" money to help increase profits. They also help draft regulations, in truth, to create barriers to entry for new and smaller competitors.

Don De Angelo

The Import/Export Bank is an unnecessary bureaucracy to help the well off. It takes money out of the public coffers to ease the business expenses of very rich companies. Whenever someone suggest closing it down the stories come out about mom-and-pop operations who can't compete in the international markets without government money. We will hear about those socialist countries who create a disadvantage for our enterprises.

If mom and pop cannot afford to compete in the world market, then they need to concentrate on domestic customers. Large corporations should get use to the expense as a normal cost of doing business. If foreign companies are receiving so much help from their governments that it results in a type of "dumping" into our market, then let the US impose a punitive tariff. The idea that the average taxpayer should be subsidizing major corporations is silly. The only companies under federal regulation should be publicly traded and/or financed corporations.

The bottom line for us as voters – we need to realize that the *Green New Deal* and the official response to COVID-19 were and are nothing more than corporate welfare on an epic scale. History will show that this past decade saw the largest wealth transfer from the poor and middle class to the already wealthy, ever!

Federal Land – Indian Land

This has been a bugaboo for many for a very long time. Most people living on the East Coast of the United States will not have as much of an opinion as those out West because the federal government doesn't own a lot of Eastern property. Over half

The American Revolution

of western land is held by all of us. Disputes over access to and uses of such land has clogged many federal courts for at least a century.

Every time a president wants to demonstrate that they care about the environment they set aside land for some special purpose. We start a new national park or nature preserve or create is a new reclamation project or breeding habitat. There may be very good reasons to do something. Anyone who goes into a national park and is not spiritually moved has no soul. But the unfettered power of the federal government to take land away and put it to whatever use is an abuse of power.

Meanwhile, the state of our Indian communities continues to suffer. The history of the abuse goes back to the very founding of European settlements, but that perpetuated on western tribes is particularly damning because we supposedly had learned our lesson and were going to redeem ourselves by treating these tribes better.

The Dawes Severalty Act was referred to as the Indian Homestead Act by those who considered themselves reformers. The white Congress decided that the Indian tribes would be broken up into separate homesteads of anywhere from 80-160 acres. Any remaining land would be turned over to the federal government for sale to the public (which lands would be left for the government would be determined by a federal agent – who would always have the best interest of the Indians in mind of course). After full assimilation, Indians would be offered full citizenship in the United States.

The Indians themselves did not want this. They were not farmers or ranchers and did not want to become separated from their fellow tribesmen. They were angry because their tribal lands had

Don De Angelo

been decimated by war and ceding their land to Americans in various treaties that the U.S. continually broke.

The solution, according to our government, was to have the Bureau of Indian Affairs (BIA) manage the land on behalf of these families --- leasing the properties out to white ranchers and farmers. The money earned was to be held in "trust" for those Indian families that opened their property for such activity. The result was a complete denial by the federal government that any such money ever existed.

See, yet another "trust fund" that never really existed. Monies taken in by the Indian leases were simply added to the other revenues and then some of that money was used by the BIA to give essentially welfare payments to remaining tribes and reservations. Indians were finally offered citizenship in 1924.

If you want to know what the U.S. economy would look like under socialism, just go onto one of these reservations. Note the abject poverty, the high rates of addiction and violence. More importantly, observe the sense of ennui and the struggle to retain cultural dignity. These are our fellow Americans. Kept in many cases in a constant state of economic malaise. Individual Indians and tribes have spent millions of dollars suing the federal government for restitution and even when they agreed to allow the U.S. to give back land in lieu of payment, the government continues to drag its feet. It is a national embarrassment.

Why do we keep fighting over what to do with public lands when there are thousands of our fellow citizens desperate to re-establish their tribal identity and economic self-sufficiency? The National Parks preserves and reserves should be turn over to those Indian tribes we stole them from in the first place. Remaining federal lands should be ceded to the states.

The American Revolution

It will not be an easy transfer, but those lands will be treated more preciously by those who see those lands as sacred than any government agency that sees them as a job. The income earned will provide careers for tribal members and end the need for a BIA. It is time to make amends and to offload millions of acres of land the government should never have held onto in the first place.

Why do this?
When the Constitution was drafted, it divided the leading men of our nation. The compromises they constructed were meant to hold a divergent set of citizens together against all odds. No one had ever posited that a government could function solely by the will of those who are governed. To make this work, the federal government – which most of the Framers knew would be the farthest removed from the people – should have a limited number of powers.

When the Federalist James Madison realized that his fellow compatriots were using a single phrase of the document – the *Necessary and Proper Clause* --to assume several additional powers not intended, he switched his allegiances and became a Democratic-Republican. The idea behind a written constitution came from an Enlightenment ideal that a "social contract" existed between a government and its people. It was not enough to trust an unwritten constitution, such as existed in England. The word "contract" was chosen specifically because it was something permanent in law. Once agreed upon a contract was permanently binding.

The idea that a contract was not to be broken was why Jefferson believed it justified America's drive for independence – the King had failed to live up to the contract, even one unwritten.

Don De Angelo

This is something that must be rediscovered by today's Americans. Even John Marshall, the Great Chief Justice who expanded federal power over 34 years on the Supreme Court, believed that contracts could never be changed.

To put it in a more simplistic manner – suppose you sign a work contract. Let's say that in this contract your employer promised to keep you employed for the next three years so long as you live up to the terms of that contract. If the employer needs to "break" this contract, they agreed to compensate you for lost pay. Now suppose that in a year or two your employer came and told you that times had changed, and they were not going to honor your contract – they were in a sense "reinterpreting" what their obligations were under that contract. Virtually anyone would sue that company, and most likely win.

What people like Ron Paul have been trying to convey to all of us is that the U.S. Constitution is the ultimate contract. It was written in 1787 as an agreement between our government and those who were to hold the ultimate sovereignty – us! When that document was being ratified many states almost rejected it because it was seen as shaky on protecting the rights of the states who had fought very hard to gain independence. The Tenth Amendment was added by Madison to ensure the states that they would hold the larger balance of (*Reserved*) governmental powers.

The struggle over slavery proved to many that state power was a greater threat to the idea of an American Union than any potential tyranny of the federal government. Since then, the national government's powers have expanded exponentially. Except for the Progressive Amendments (XVI -- XIX), most of this power

The American Revolution

has been grabbed under a very loose interpretation of the federal government's power to regulate interstate commerce.

The expanding federal power has drawn sovereignty away from families, communities, and states and concentrated it in a national regime. It doesn't matter which party is in power the same players control how the economy will function, how many wars we will fight, and who among us will get the sympathy and support of the government's largess.

Do you ever wonder why big banks and large corporations seem to dominate public life? Do you get frustrated when you realize that you might be sending lots of money to Washington, DC only to see trickles of it coming back to your community with all sorts of strings attached? Do you feel as though you are talking but no one seems to be listening? Even the media seems to be concentrated in a few large corporations who have become the mouthpieces of specific political ideologies. Your observations are correct, but your explanation might be misguided.

People will always choose to obtain more power -- even good people. They see others suffering and decide they need to act. To act they need to have the power to make decisions. To wait for the Constitution to be amended becomes seen as an impediment to progress. It is easier to reinterpret the Constitution than amend it. If enough hardship falls on enough Americans, they panic and acquiesce to federal grabs for additional power. The idealism here is underscored in the New Deal greeting, "I am from the federal government, and I am here to help."

The aftermath of this power concentration has created an economy that is not really a free market and a republic that is under attack by a thousand referendums. We have lots of things to vote on but never feel like we have control over anything.

The New Dealers of the 1930s came under fire in the 1950s as having harbored communist and socialist ideas. The truth is that many of them were indeed hopeful of a socialist revolution in America. Stalin's actions in the Soviet Union and Eastern Europe, the disillusionment among these individuals was significant. The conservative wave that dominated the 1950s, like all movements, lost its steam by 1960. John F. Kennedy was seen by many Americans as an acceptable moderate option.

The former socialist activists, having been locked out of the political dialogue for over a decade needed a new message. The New Left emerged to challenge the status quo. The turbulent years at the end of the 1960s reflect this frustration by those who believed that a free market, republic was not capable of providing a good life for most of its people. Saul Allinski, an anti-Stalinist Marxist, wrote *Rules for Radicals* as a blueprint for leftist. He essentially encourages his followers to turn their attentions to infiltrating the existing system – education, law, corporate investing, journalism, and the favorite, community organizing.

The poor and working classes needed to be educated and unified against the existing system because they were being abused by it. In this book he explains that when helping the poor every tactic used was fair game. He equated his struggle as a "war" and because he was on the right side of the issues, he did not have to follow the normal rules. If this doesn't sound familiar to you, please read Barack Obama's biography. His only work experience

The American Revolution

before joining the state senate of Illinois was as a community organizer. It sounds innocuous to the average ear because it sounds like people helping other people to take care of themselves. It really means teaching community groups (ones that share your political ideology) to petition the federal government for more programs, money, and attention.

It becomes a self-perpetuating system. Community groups beckon for federal help, they become dependent on that help, and then vote only for those politicians who will support those programs. Public employees who need a large government to secure their jobs, form unions who will collect dues and use that money to help elect those same politicians. Even corporate executives will jump on this train. Get cozy with the right politician, who will earmark support for these programs, and you have a guaranteed customer. If you make your company specialize in government work, you can gain a virtual monopoly. The same thing happens on the right as well. Become a defense contractor and you can more easily manipulate your market by lobbying just 536 people sitting in Washington, DC. The *Iron Triangle* is a solid reality in the country and needs to be brought under control if not ended.

The 2024 election is not about who is the better American. It is not about the person with the best personality. It is about what direction the American people want for the nation. We have been able to kick this can down the road for a very long time. It has been a wonderful ride for the most part. The elites always have their power and access to wealth, which only increases in times of crisis because they can afford to buy up the loses of average Americans who must sell cheaply to stay afloat. But the easy part is over. Regardless of the choice we make there will be hardship. There is no other option.

Don De Angelo

THE CHOICES

The main reason why you feel like nothing changes is really because we do not like to hear that we must make a real choice and then live with the consequences. We like government on the cheap. If someone is offering you something for free, why would you later agree to pay for it? Both parties play the game because we let them. Remember, we elect our representatives – they reflect us.

The Libertarian Option: wants to offer you the freedom that is talked about in the Enlightenment and Great Awakening philosophy that virtually all the Founders and Framers embraced. The government will be small, will do only those things listed in Article I, Section VIII. The basis of this platform depends on individual liberty and individual responsibility. The main axiom of this perspective is a neo-Kennedy call to, "ask not what your country can do for you, ask what you can do for yourself and your fellow man."

The utopian vision of mankind is rejected and instead embraces what Madison referred to as the natural proclivity of mankind to pursue their own interest(s). The free society guaranteed by the Constitution provides a series of checks and balances that allows these conflicting interests to find some common ground when necessary or at other times to coexist peacefully. This has been historically called *pluralism*.

Public schools will have to compete with private and parochial ones to find the best provider of education. Egalitarianism will mean that everyone can pursue their own happiness and rise as far as their abilities will take them. Inherent in this is the reality that some will fail. Private charity, which provides the

The American Revolution

most efficient and compassionate help, will have to pick up the slack. Less government means more personal and community effort. Less government means more freedom, but freedom always comes at a cost.

If you vote Libertarian this fall you are saying that you want the government to live up to the strictest interpretation of the Constitution and you are supporting the notion that the federal government must be significantly reduced in size and power. You want the Supreme Court to start interpreting the laws and not use their rulings to create new law. You will be saying with your vote that you want the Constitution to be seen as a "contract" and not a "living document" that can change upon the whims of whomever has power at any given time – *Judicial Originalism*. The bottom line with Libertarianism is -- More freedom, more uncertainty – the axiom of Benjamin holds true: "those who will sacrifice some of their liberty for temporary security, deserve neither liberty nor security."

The Republican Option: With the Republicans you get much of what is above but also supporting a foreign policy that is very aggressive and interventionist. You will be expected to finance multiple, undeclared wars of choice and tolerate a considerable amount of death and destruction done in your name. This will add billions if not trillions of additional spending, not to mention increasing animosity towards Americans. There are no party commitments to balanced budgets in the establishment Republican party and more. The debt is only bad when it is for liberal projects, but the military industrial complex will always deserve more spending.

If the Trump "vision" for America becomes the new standard of the Republican party, you will see more protectionism and

Don De Angelo

isolationism. While we will continue to fight wars with people who have not directly attacked us, mini wars of choice will continue if not expand. While there will be more corporate welfare to supposedly encourage more hiring, and we won't be doing much trading with anyone. These policies will increase the cost of living and antagonize many of our traditional allies around the world.

The Democratic Option: is based upon the notion that only the federal government can guarantee the success of the American people. When Mr. Obama said that he wants to spread the success of America's wealth, he is coining a new phrase to mean income redistribution. The platform is based on the idea that people and society can be forced to behave in certain ways and that those educated in the elite schools of American can best decide what is best for all of us. The Democrats want to help people by ending suffering, poverty, and violence. They have embraced a progressive notion that the human condition is kept back by elements out of human control. To ensure success, there needs a champion to show them the proper direction. Because the states are too diverse there must be one center of control to ensure equal outcomes. This is a classical federalist ideology.

Cass Sunstein, the president Obama's czar of domestic regulatory policy wrote a book, *Nudge*, which basically states that the government must study the proper behavior required to better society. Once that behavior is determined the government can force people into the better lifestyle by essentially eliminating their *options*, by which they mean freedoms, so that they think they are choosing this better behavior.[66] Don't think this is hap-

---

66   https://www.youtube.com/watch?v=Rewo7dPiRyU The idea that government must limit choices in order to "nudge" you into making better decisions is important to understand what is really meant by a truly "Nanny State."

The American Revolution

pening? Look back at the last three years (2020-2023). We were nudged by propaganda and outright lies to lock ourselves down, take an untested vaccine, and damage the long-term intellectual and personal lives of an entire generation of young people. They did this without firing a shot. Our government did this with our money, and a ton of debt that our children and grandchildren will have to pay. The elites of both parties and every corporation now assume it is their right to do this because we did not resist. In fact, most of us ridiculed those few who did. They were canceled, de-platformed, labeled traitors and a threat to human life. Family members excommunicated those of their own blood because they were "unvaxxed."

Franklin Roosevelt began this thinking with his "Brain Trust" in the 1930s. He surrounded himself with PhDs from Ivy League institutions and they essentially wrote his speeches and designed the New Deal programs. Today, the president surrounds himself with his fellow elite school graduates and believes that they know what's best for the nation. If you see yourself as a helpless victim, then the Democratic Party is your choice. They will try very hard to take care of you and make sure that you are not victimized again. This is why the Democrats are in lock step with the World Economic Forum's Great Reset. *You will own nothing, and you will be happy!*

If you vote Democrat, you are saying that you want to give up additional freedoms for a stronger sense of security. It will not necessarily be the security you are thinking of but what the government determines the best level security for most people. You are saying that you are willing to follow rules established by "professional" bureaucrats on even the most minor aspects of your life. Think of the law to make buying incandescent light bulbs illegal. Consider the ever-expanding list of vaccines you child *must* have to attend school. You are saying that you are willing to limit your options in many areas of your life to ensure that some level of benefit will be available to all.[67]

The Green Party Option: If you like the idea of more fairness and equality of outcomes (equity), then the Green party is for you. This is the true socialist party in America. The Green party began in Europe as an anti-nuclear movement, partly financed by the Soviet Union. Since the end of the Cold War, it has expanded to address all issues of environmental concern. It has also incorporated the idea of shared economies to lessen suffering of the poor and mandate equal economic and social outcomes.

There is a Social Democrat Association in the United States, but it is mainly focused on pushing their ideas onto the Democrat party, which isn't quite the same. The Greens are at least committed to being a full-throated advocate of socialist reorganization of the U.S. system. Their platform will require considerable growth in the size and power of the federal governments. It will also permit further intrusions by state and local governments.

Where Republicans require you to take on more responsibility for your own happiness the Democrats want you to turn over your personal sovereignty so that everyone has a fairer country. Where Republicans tell you that their system has no human cost the Democrats say there is no cost at all to those making less than $250,000. Both are dishonest.

By saying yes to the Democratic Party platform, you are agreeing to pay a significant amount of your income and saving's

---

67   https://democrats.org

The American Revolution

interest in taxes. If Greece has taught us anything it is that you cannot have a cradle-to-grave socialist system on the cheap. The tax rates in Greece are 50%, and they are on the verge of bankruptcy. President Obama promised no taxes on 95% of Americans, but his $1.5 trillion annual deficits say that is not sustainable. The bill will eventually come due and then the taxes will have to go up for all of us. You could confiscate all the wealth of the top 1% and only cover this next year's deficit – then what?

Let me be clear. This may be exactly what the American people want. They may really believe that this utopian vision of America is possible and desirable. But we need to be clear that this America has nothing to do with the one envisioned by our Founding Fathers and Framers. A president who can expand federal power by executive order or recess appointments has nothing to do with any part of the U.S. Constitution. If you want the president's vision for the country, you are saying that you essentially want to ditch the Constitution and start over again. This is the president's essential message. When Barack Obama says that he wants to, "fundamentally transform America," he is not kidding. He is saying that the America as defined by the Constitution has failed and the nation must turn to him and the Democratic Party for its salvation. There is no discussion of amending the document or even replacing it. Either of these options would require a super majority support of the American people, which they will never get. So, it is all about "reinterpreting" the document to find powers necessary to concentrate all government authority in Washington, DC – and more specifically the presidency. This will render the Constitution meaningless. The result will either be a call for a convention to draft and new document or a breakdown of the system without a new framework – chaos.

Don De Angelo

The choice is stark, and the consequences are grave. The choices we make in will permanently change the nation. Hopefully we are all up to the task and I pray that we will all take the process more seriously than the media that have already made its choice.

So, what is there to do?

I believe that this election is critical to the success of the nation. It will determine what kind of country we will live in and which our posterity will inherit. Elections are always a pain. At some point, none of the candidates seem appealing. The constant campaign ads and debates make the whole process appear unseemly. But this is the system we have, and we must embrace it. This requires us to rise above the fray and take the voting responsibility serious.

My strongest suggestion is to look to the party platforms rather than the candidates. No matter what level – congressmen, senators, governors, or president – find out what they stand for rather than how they look or sound.

I have given you the good and the bad of both parties and it is time that all of us pick our poison. If you want the Democratic vision for America, then vote Democrat all the way down the ballot. If you want the Republican system in place, then it's the opposite choice. The important thing is that you do it and live with your choice. Whoever gets elected will need at least two years to get the ball rolling. Vote and then give your full support to the winner.

For years, I have struggled with my personal views. From the age of 18 until my late 20s I was a registered non-partisan

The American Revolution

because I wanted to remain "independent". I voted for Ronald Reagan but also voted for Patrick Moynihan to be my Senator (one of the most liberal persons to sit in the Senate). I voted for Senator Lieberman when I lived in Connecticut.

But when I heard Bill Clinton campaign in 1992, I knew that the Democratic Party was going in a distinctly Marxist direction. I really do feel that this is a perfectly fine position to have but it is one that I personally find incompatible with the Constitution and the principle of a free people. I registered as a Republican. But that decision began to bug me as the Republican Party began to expand the role of the federal government as well. They wanted a smaller government except when it comes to the military and the social issues that they care about. You cannot be for small government and then ask the government to start regulating personal liberties. I am a strongly religious person but that is my personal business.

Voting Libertarian has proven to be more of a protestation than an actual position. The media's attempts to force Americans to only consider two options is, in fact, and attempt to help the Democrat party get and sustain power. A Marxist media for a Marxist government. They refuse to be honest about that because, as Marxist bent on revolution, they don't need to be truthful. Victory at all costs because they are convinced of their righteousness. Marxists use terms like "lived truth" or the post-modern "there is no objective truth." They cannot be honest of their intent because they know it would be rejected, so it must be accomplished by deceit.

Living in a nation with very little government does make me nervous. I am not so confident in my abilities that I don't fear being left to fend for myself. But I want to live as free a life as I can.

Don De Angelo

I don't want to live in a country where someday the government can come in and tell which doctor I use or what job I take or which schools my children can attend. I want to try living with a government that lives within the confines of the Constitution. I believe that if Americans are told that they need to pick themselves up and make their own lives better – they will. It won't happen overnight, and some people will fall between the cracks – but we will know liberty in its more, pure form.

I will respect my fellow Americans if they decide that another option is the way to go. I will find a way to be successful in a system with fewer options and more expensive taxation. If I ever find that life in a country, no longer based on the Constitution is too much for me to bear then I must find somewhere else to live. Tragically I do not know where liberty still lives unencumbered.

PART IV

Options And Choices

Don De Angelo

It can be very helpful to have a synopsis of what has been laid out to be clear. There are always choices and before we make them it is always good to be sure we understand the options. It is also good to realize that regardless of what path we pursue there are some things that we must do locally and personally regardless. My suggestion in this book is to return to the founding principles of the United States Constitution and apply them to our contemporary problems. The main reason for this is that we are at a place where very modern *liberals* and *conservatives* are not always aligned with what most of us have accepted as established truth. Going back to standards from long ago might allow all sides to embrace a rebalancing of power in the country. If there can be no consensus, then the next set of options can only be described as various means of *amiable divorce*.

The two remaining options are even more dire. The last four years have exposed the neo-Marxist agenda of global elites. Whether it is the *One World* aspirations of the United Nations or the *Great Reset* of the World Economic Forum, surrendering our national identity and individual sovereignty to such a fate is an option. This would ultimately lead to the final option, which is a civil war.

In all the possibilities, we the people have obligations to ourselves and our communities to act. Strong individuals forming voluntary associations (regardless of what you call them) is the only guarantee of survival regardless of which path we choose to take as a nation. Creating SHEW Associations are a primary example. They must be centered around either a faith community, social affiliation, or through established interest groups. In the system being promoted here this is done through the dissolution of federal power down to the local level. These would be tax

The American Revolution

exempt groups that would get there funding from the people. Everyone would give 10% of their income every payday to the association of their choice. Their flat-rate income tax would be based on their net income *after* their contribution.

If communities can handle those most-basic needs, then what happens in the rest of the world become less critical. If I can feed myself, I am less vulnerable to market forces and even less dependent on government largess. The more independent the community, the less those citizens are beholden to a distant and unresponsive federal regime. The more my tax dollars remain closest to me the more control I have over how it is spent. Keeping the federal revenue stream limited to a VAT and/or sales tax should force it to control spending. Nothing is fool proof. A nation of people determined to drive off a cliff will find a way to press the gas pedal.

Option 1: Restore True Federalism

When the Framers completed their work in Philadelphia, most were not sure they could even get their contemporaries to embrace it. The idea that one could establish a body politic based on the sovereign power of the people was novel. All the Founding Fathers feared democracy and put in place a system of checks-and-balances to try and prevent a tyranny of either a majority or a violent minority. History told many of them to go forward with the understanding that it might not work. When Thomas Jefferson read it, he gave it 20 years before needing to be vigorously altered or abandoned all together. For this option to work, at least four major constitutional amendments will

Don De Angelo

be required. After these adjustments, the main work of tearing down unnecessary and bloated federal institutions must take place. The result will be a federal system that divides government power among the national, state, and local entities in a manner that respects the diversity of political ideologies that have emerged without sacrificing the democratic republic that guarantees individual liberty.

To ensure that the federal government can never again assume additional powers that are best handled at the state and local levels; the United States Senate must be a permanent voice for the state governments. The 28th Amendment should repeal the 17th Amendment. All US Senators should be the appointees of the state legislatures. This sends democracy purist through the roof. The sole purpose of the Senate was to protect the powers of the states from the ever-encroaching interference of the federal government. Without that mechanism, the smaller states would never have ratified the Constitution.

The argument for the 17th Amendment was that the US Senate had become a *millionaire's club*, too far detached from the people. If we allowed the voters to elect their senators directly, we would end such elitism and abuse. The current US Senate is not only loaded with billionaires and millionaires; most of its members obtained their wealth FROM being in the Senate. Meanwhile, the federal government has used this institutional *reform* to grab additional powers not originally expressed in the Constitution. It has also created mini fiefdoms for those senators who can keep their seats. One senator can halt progress, not for the good of their state or its people: but solely for their own gain. Returning the Senate to one reflective of the will of the state legislatures is a major check against unchecked expansion of federal power.

The American Revolution

The next amendment deals with fiscal responsibility. The 29th Amendment would be called the Budget Process Amendment. There is a lot of blame that can be placed on the doorsteps of both parties when it comes to fiscal irresponsibility. But the truth of the matter is that there is *no constitutional directive on how the budget must be derived*, except to say that all tax and spending matters must originate in the House of Representatives. The only way to bring the budgets under control and begin to pay off the national debt is to spell out specifically how to put a budget together.

The first element of the amendment would be to have the House of Representatives draft a two-year budget for the years after their term. The Congress that sits between 2025 and 2027, would draft the budget for 2026-2028. This way the actual spending of the money would happen *after* another election. Congressmen and Congresswomen who pass pork-laden budgets will have to explain that to their constituents *before* the money is spent. The budget would then go to the Senate for either approval, rejection, or alterations. If rejected or corrected the budget goes back to the House. If the House does not like the Senate's proposals, there is a mandatory *Conference Committee* made up of the leadership of all parties from both houses. A *compromise budget* is drafted and then sent back to both houses for a straight up-or-down vote.

The budget would be sent to the president for signature. The president should have a *line-item veto* to avoid all-or-nothing scenarios. In such cases a two-thirds vote in both houses would override the president's decision.

Failure to meet the deadline for a budget would result in a halt in pay for all federal employees, including members of the

Don De Angelo

Congress. This would be for every day the budget is late and any missed paydays will *not* be made up. The president is given full control over how incoming revenue is spent.

All appropriation bills would be handled in the same way. A great start to this process would be an agreement to have the first two years of transition (2025-2027 for instance) be a locked in budget based on 2018 spending (the year before COVID). This would bring in more tax revenue than budgeted – that's correct a budget surplus.

The amendment must also make it law that all budgets must be balanced unless there is a formal state of war or a declared national emergency by the president. This would require a two-thirds vote of both houses. In the hoped for result of a surplus, the federal government has prescribed options. The priority is to pay off the national debt. The government may deem it necessary to purchase gold to stabilize the currency and this would also be permitted. Surpluses may also be applied to a *sovereign wealth fund* established by the US Treasury Department.

The 30th Amendment would be the Judicial Reform Amendment. The first provision would require all federal judges to be at least 50 years of age. The mandatory age for a Supreme Court justice should be 60. No one on the Supreme Court should be permitted to serve for more than 15 years, with a mandatory retirement of 75. The next element is more controversial but necessary to avoid returning to the acrimony we currently see over Court opinions.

The core of disputes among judicial scholars and activists is the philosophical perspectives of the sitting justices. Those who believe that the federal government should have whatever powers

The American Revolution

they deem *necessary and proper* are referred to as judicial activists. People who feel that federal power should be strictly limited to the expressed powers in Article I, Section VIII prefer the Court to exercise judicial restraint. The problem is that restraint when it comes to individual liberty should never be encouraged; and no free society can exist under activist government. The remedy is to apply the best method of constitutional interpretation to the appropriate legal scenarios.

The federal courts must apply strict construction to all decisions regarding government power. This would mean a literal interpretation of the Tenth Amendment, often referred to as the States' Rights Amendment. Any assumption of additional power by the federal government outside of the *expressed powers* should be rejected. Likewise, the federal courts must apply loose construction to any issue of individual liberty. This would be a liberal interpretation of the Ninth Amendment, also known as the Unenumerated Rights Amendment. There would still be flexibility in how such opinions would be expressed in the laws; but would bring many long-standing disputes over Court decision-making to an end.

The final amendment deals with the most consequential power of any government – the declaration of war. The 31st Amendment would be the War Powers Amendment. Since World War II, the United States has seen its fighting men and women deployed to every corner of the world. While not always in the spirit of empire; the American military has often acted with imperial zeal and criminal behavior. The larger issue is the opportunity for suspension of civil liberties and the intrusion of the government into our lives. The cost of such behavior has contributed to most of the national debt.

Don De Angelo

The first provision must be to end the use of resolutions when approving the use of military assets. These *authorizations to use force* are non-legally binding expressions of the congressional will that provide cover for politicians. As explained earlier, Congress gives the authorization and if the president succeeds, they take credit for giving the green light. If the deployment end in catastrophe, the same person can argue that they never intended for the president to take such reckless abuse of their license. Meanwhile billions of dollars are wasted every day and countless lives of lost or damaged. The new rule should be simple: Any war must be a formally declared vote of the Congress. My personal preference is that it must be a two-thirds vote of both houses.

The amendment would be making the War Powers Act a constitutional formality. The president acting as Commander-in-Chief may deploy the military for 90 days to address any national security issue. Within that period, the president must issue a written statement to the Congress for a formal declaration of war. If no such war message is submitted, or if it is rejected by congressional vote, the president has 90 days to recall the military. The Congress may issue an extension of military operations under situations where demobilization would prove dangerous to our personnel or sensitive equipment. Such extensions have the approval of Congress, with the filibuster applicable in the US Senate.

The next phase of reform would entail the dismantling of the juggernaut we call the federal bureaucracy. The easiest departments for elimination would be those that will be assumed by the states and/or local governments. The departments of education, housing, welfare, and agriculture should immediately go within the first two years (to accommodate the two-year budget

The American Revolution

process explained above). The more aggressive cutting the better. The departments of energy, interior, and environmental protection would make my list as well.

There is another grouping of departments that need removal but for more nefarious reasons. The Central Intelligence Agency (CIA) and the Federal Bureau of Investigations (FBI) are at the top of this list. These would be best described as *departments of liberty killers*. The CIA and FBI should be broken up and brought under the control of other departments or agencies. Foreign intelligence in all its forms should be placed in the Department of Foreign Affairs. The rest should just go away. The investigation element of the FBI should be placed under the US Marshall and the rest gone for good. End the *War on Drugs* and the DEA and ATF could disappear.

Following suggestions from an earlier chapter and the Bureau of Indian Affairs is gone. One could also argue that the existence of the Federal Communications Commission is anachronistic and wasteful. Once one gets started there is just so much fat to cut.

The next area for savings is federal lands. There is no reason for the government to own land, except for military bases, which it is required to have to not violate the Third Amendment. As suggested earlier, national parks and preserves should be offered to the local Indian tribes. As long as there is continued open access for all Americans and visiting tourists, this is a great gesture of reconciliation. There will be fighting among the tribes over who had the land first; but that is why we have civil courts. National forests, reserves and other holdings should be ceded to the states in which they exist. Now the Department of the Interior can disappear, and the *Bureau of Historical Landmarks* can operate under the Department of Domestic Affairs.

Don De Angelo

So called *government corporations* and *independent agencies* should be auctioned off to the highest bidders. The Tennessee Valley Authority would sell quickly and maybe sell NASA. AMTRAK and the United States Postal Service might be tougher sells but why not? If these entities are so important to the commercial function of the nation, then private enterprise will run them more efficiently and effectively.

The next group fall under the *feel good about us* category. The National Endowment of the Arts, Humanities and Sciences all must be privatized. My proposal is to make an additional one-billion-dollar *endowment* to each in year one and then they are on their own. If the public do not see the value in spending money on these enterprises, so be it. It would also benefit society to see these programs adopted into existing universities.

The real test is to take a few moments to and look up the shear number of departments, agencies, and bureaus of the federal regime. There is simply no rationale for it all. Most of these programs were begun as responses to *emergencies* that never intended to have permanent government infrastructures. Others have duplicate entities that should be handling the matter. The remaining are pure power grabs by the federal government with the intention of intruding on personal liberties. To rid ourselves of such bloated offices will earn much needed fiscal relief and expand freedom for all Americans.

Option 2: Amiable Divorces

Breaking up is always hard to do, according to Neil Sedaka and probably anyone else who experiences it firsthand. When nations

The American Revolution

fall apart it is far more traumatic because of the sheer numbers of people impacted. But when a society has come to a place where two factions cannot even agree on one set of facts of principles, it is impossible to see how to stay together. The remaining decision seems to be *how* to part amiably and perhaps hope of future cooperation based on mutual histories and cultural ties. The next question is determining how to separate and under which conditions. One obvious calculation is that the $32+ trillion debt gets divided and which military assets goes to which entity. The bottom line should be to prioritize the *peaceful transfer* to whatever new reality is to be created.

Historically the political divide in the country has fallen into two main camps. Traditional *federalists* have been those who support a strong central government to act as an *umpire* over the states to ensure uniformity in national priorities and protection of individual freedoms. The opposing *antifederalist* position is that states retain most of the governing powers, which have been reserved to them by the US Constitution. While it is still true that most Americans are probably still in either camp; there is a very vocal minority on both sides that make *statism* and priority for some and *anarchism* for others. What we have come to call the *Red/Blue Divide* has now morphed into a more complex, *Red/Blue/Purple/Pink* one. In Option 1, where local governments control the SHEW business, this can happen without resentment or rivalry. However, statists require *one* government entity imposing one agenda for everyone and again it is hard to see where there can ever be one agreed upon set of standards that would make anyone happy. If this is struggle persists, it will only become more contentious and violent unless there is a peaceful separation.

Don De Angelo

This is *not* the preferred outcome. The first option was laid out specifically because it is, in my opinion the only way to keep the nation together while respecting the fact that Americans can and do have differing preferences on how they are governed. We need also remember that the breakup of the United States will not be like the *Velvet Divorce* of Czechoslovakia, but more akin to the collapse of the Soviet Union. Both were essentially bloodless but ending the USSR was a realignment of the entire globe that became destabilizing for literally millions of people. The breakup of the world's greatest superpower is no small thing, and those who think that the destruction of the *American Empire* will be universal blessing to the human flourishing are delusional. Regardless of the historical and practical realities that may or may not arise, it would be equally irresponsible to keep assuming that the United States will always stay together and that nothing could challenge its status in world affairs.

To make a practical application of the various manifestations of this course of action, we will focus on a *Red v. Blue* reality. But the next question will be *in what context* will the separation occur? There is always the risk that once the country starts dividing itself that other demands for further divisions be acceptable; the focus here is to three obvious possibilities and then one somewhat crazy outcome.

Red State Blue State seems the most plausible as it is the current subdivision of the country. It is also how we currently describe the political divisions whenever we hold an election. In this scenario the nation would separate according to essentially *federalist* and *antifederalist* nations. In this breakup, the red states would either go entirely independent or join with each other in a loose confederation like our original constitution. Washington,

The American Revolution

DC would remain the capital of the blue states and how they choose to *interpret* the Constitution.

Those "red people" trapped in a "blue nation" would be forced to accept this reality and peacefully participate in the body politic to keep the drive to centralized power as slow and unintrusive as possible. Likewise, the "blue people" in a "red nation" would find it difficult to insist on one having a collective rule for the entire country. Because of this dilemma, it seems that one might try to avoid *pockets of resistance* within newly created political entities.

<u>Red County Blue County</u> would address the needs of those political minorities stranded in new countries with which they do not agree. In this scenario a plebiscite would be needed because there is no constitutional accommodation for dividing states into smaller units without the consent of the people. The first question would be "which interpretation of the Constitution is desired?" Those counties that support the Constitution as it is written (strict construction) would be the *Red People* and those who hold onto loose construction (living document) would be the *Blues*. In this case, the red states would remain the United States and those who believe that the Constitution is a flawed document that needs constant reinterpretations would be a new entity free to keep the document with flexible readings or ditch it entirely and construct something entirely new.

The issue here is one of physical disparity. There are plenty of ways to view what a division of the Union in this manner would look. The blue counties would essentially be cities with vast swathes of red territory. *If those cities were not willing or able to be fully independent,* it might be very difficult to form the *uniform* political system their political philosophy supports. Imagine the difficulty in choosing a capital for such a union, let alone

230

enforcing one set a law in such a disparate collection of urban enclaves.

Red State Blue Cities is an interesting possibility because it could happen in either a divorced United States or as a preserved Union, if the political structure of such a realignment of American political units is based on strict construction of the US Constitution. (See Option 1). Now we would have two possible outcomes. In the first, all the states would be red, and cities would be designated as a *Blue Nation-State.* Here the multiple cities would share just one central government to formulate public policy for all. One could imagine a physically central location, such as St. Louis, MO, as the place where decisions were made, while the cities themselves would enforce or execute the law. I would label this the *satellite centralization* formula.

The red states would remain the United States of America with its capital, Washington, DC. There could be an agreement to keep a shared currency or a redefined North American Free Trade Area; and there would need to be a strong agreement on possible shared defenses. In this respect you would no longer have a singular American superpower; but perhaps this would preserve a perceived union of strength, which would deter enemy plots against our collective security.

The alternative formation would keep the Union together but with *two* governing systems. The red states would continue to operate under a strict interpretation of the Constitution and the blue cities would function as *federal entities.* The federal areas would follow the law as enacted by Congress and would not have any local government. This would afford these populations to live under a centralized decision-making structure without imposing on the states that prefer devolved power.

The American Revolution

This would mean separate representation of the blue cities in both houses and remove revenue from cities to be collected by the states in which they are located. The red states would have to accept two senators from each city, which would cause quite a bit of resistance. This could be mitigated by having each blue city made up of larger physical areas. Picture a large *city* called *New England* that stretched from Newark, NY to Boston, MA. The beauty of this of course is keeping the physical body called the United States of America together.

The Crazy Version of this option would be to expand this concept to include Canada. Recent events have seen similar rural/urban disunity in Canada. In my silly spin on this tune the blue cities of the United States and Canada would be linked to the province of Ontario and would all be called Canada, with the capital of Ottawa. The red areas of both would be called the United States of America with the capital of Washington, DC. The only reason for this construct is the desire to avoid mass migration of people to desired *new territory.* It is certainly a harder sell in Canada, which has historically (for good reason) repelled any movement in this direction. Should Justin Trudeau hold on to power much longer and drive his country further down the path of globalist agendas, there could be a major shift in that reluctance.

Option 3: Surrender to the Marxist Agenda of Global Elites

One might already detect the direction of this analysis. However, there may be a genuine desire on the part of most Americans to subjugate our national priorities to that of the United Nations (UN), or more specifically the World Economic Forum (WEF).

Don De Angelo

This seems ridiculous until one realizes that the World Health Organization (WHO) is currently attempting to get all nations to give the WHO (not the band) complete sovereignty over the entire world when it comes to dealing with *global health emergencies*. The WEF is recommending the same practice regarding climate and immigration rules.

The implementation of this option would require a complete abrogation of the existing constitution. While it has become a varsity sport in Washington to see just how far the *Elastic Clause* can be stretched without breaking, it is impossible to infer that the necessary and proper use of power for the federal government could ever mean surrendering its sovereignty to a foreign entity.

It is difficult how this would happen under our current political environment. Red state people, already angry at too much centralized policy in Washington, would be in open rebellion if forced to obey any *world government*. Option 3 becomes more of a precursor to Option 2, regardless of which version is chosen.

Option 4: Civil War II: The Sequel
There is little to be said as such an outcome is too shameful to consider and too awful to imagine. For that reason, I will fight for Option 1, while I prepare to deal with Option 2. In case of Option 3, I would become an expatriate.

It also very important to understand a critical point of this option: There will be very few bystanders. The next US Civil War will be a fight for global domination. Who sides with whom would be an interesting set of bedfellows. The conflagration would be apocalyptic in scope and a level of death and destruction closer to Armageddon than Antietam. We should all pray and dedicate ourselves to ensure this option never becomes a viable one.

Epilogue

The exercise of sovereign power is complicated and fraught with danger. Whenever we discuss possible shifts in the existing order, we are playing with hot knives – even when we manage to keep all our limbs and fingers, it burns. To not have the discussion is to imitate other great powers of history who out of pride or denial chose to ignore the potential cataclysm staring in their faces.

It is critically important to remind ourselves of the frailty of life and the existence of political entities. The collapse of Rome was unimaginable only to those living in 400 CE. For those reading this book old enough to remember the fall of the Soviet Empire, the idea seemed mythical even as we watched the Berlin Wall disappear. Much of what younger people have lived through are because of those days – just ask the Ukrainians.

The British certainly didn't want to have their victory over Hitler to also mean the end of its empire, which was the most extensive and lucrative in human history. While the cultural and economic shocks of its decline have been painful, they seem to have been able to take it all in and adjust to a new role as a major influence in world affairs and economic trade. Wounded pride didn't seem to push the British into foolish struggles that only delayed the inevitable.

Don De Angelo

When cometh the storm? Like Abraham Lincoln, I believe that "If destruction be our lot, we must ourselves be its author and finisher. As a nation of freemen, we must live through all time, or die by suicide."[68] Like many of the larger historical powers, the United States has become intrinsically tied to the most peaceful world order that has ever existed. Many sovereign powers and desperate populations around the world rely on American prowess, if not hegemony, to keep themselves afloat. While it is silly to assume that the world would rally to save us from our own foolishness; there would certainly be a strong effort to encourage us to embrace self-preservation.

We the People are a motley collection of wonderful humans. We have done great harm but have also created some of the best innovations and inventions the world has ever seen. We have entertained and healed billions but have tortured millions. The good and bad of it is a truth we must accept and then decide whether it is all worth it. My vote is to reach back to those founding principles that the whole world has venerated, and remain a United States of America.

---

68   Lincoln, Abraham *Speech to the Young Men's Lyceum of Springfield (1838)*.

A Short Reading List

Cooke, Jacob E., Editor, *The Federalist*, Alexander Hamilton, John Jay, and James Madison. Wesleyan University Press, Middleton, CT.

Drinker Bowe, Catherine, *Miracle at Philadelphia*. Atlantic Monthly Press, Boston, MA: 1966.

Onuf, Peter and Nicholas Onuf, *Federal Union, Modern World: The Law of Nations in an Age of Revolutions*. Madison House, 1993.

Onuf, Peter, *Jefferson's Empire: The Language of American Nationhood*, University Press of Virginia, Charlottesville and London, 2000.

Rakove, Jack N., *Original Meanings: Politics and Ideas in the Making of the Constitution*. Alfred A. Knopf, New York, 1996.

Solberg, Winton U., Editor, *The Constitutional Convention and the Formation of the Union*, the edited notes of James Madison from the Constitutional Convention. University of Illinois Press, Urbana and Chicago, 1990.

Don De Angelo

Storing, Herbert J., Editor, *The Anti-Federalist: Writings by the Opponents of the Constitution.* University of Chicago Press, Chicago, IL, 1981.

Veit, Helen E, Kenneth R. Rowing, et al., Editors, *Creating the Bill of Rights: The Documentary Record from the First Federal Congress.* The Johns Hopkins University Press, Baltimore, MD, 1991.

About the Author

Don De Angelo was born in Pennsylvania and raised in Western New York state. He earned his BA in International Relations from the University of Delaware in 1987 and began teaching in Stamford Connecticut. After two years Don began a five-year stint with The Chase Manhattan Bank, NA (now JP Morgan Chase) in various capacities. During that time, he earned an MA in International Relations from the University of San Diego, in 1995.

Don returned to teaching in 1996 and had a 25-year career with the University of San Diego High School/Cathedral Catholic High School. He taught AP US History for 20 years along with AP European History and AP American Government as well as World History. Don was also an assistant coach for Novice Boys Volleyball, both boys and girls Novice Water Polo, and was Head Coach for Boys and Girls Varsity and JV swimming and diving teams. De Angelo was named a Fellow of the James Madison Memorial Fellowship Foundation in 2007, which was a grant for a second MA in History. He graduated from San Diego State University in 2009. The following year, Don as inducted into the San Diego County High School Sports Hall of Fame as a "Legend of Coaching" for swimming and diving.

Don De Angelo

Throughout this period, Don was active with the San Diego County and California state Libertarian party, acting as the Vice Chair of the SDLP for four years. He also co-hosted the SDLP Podcast with Joseph De Paul, which was a weekly podcast covering local and state politics. Like many people around the world, COVID brought many tragedies and painful events. A decision to leave San Diego for a teaching assignment in Bermuda turned into a disaster. Don eventually returned to his hometown in 2022 and is a semi-retired, Adjunct Professor of History and Political Science at Jamestown Community College.

Printed in the USA
CPSIA information can be obtained
at www.ICGtesting.com
LVHW020553071224
798551LV00002B/140